Bring America Back To Her Religious Roots

A History of Our Christian Heritage

Other Materials by the Author

America's Christian Heritage

America's Exceptionalism

Are Christians Supposed to be Wealthy?

Bring America Back To Her Religious Roots

A History of Our Christian Heritage

By Roger Anghis

Edited by Lee Ann Anghis

Restore FreeSpeech Press
www.restorefreespeech.org
Littleton, Colorado

Original works Presented to:

Oral Roberts University
7777 South Lewis Avenue
Tulsa, Oklahoma 74171

Hillsdale College
33 East College Street
Hillsdale, MI 49242

WallBuilders
P.O. Box 397
Aledo, Texas 76008

NewsWithViews.com

Copyright © 2011 Roger Anghis

Cover design by:
Danny Anghis

Printed in the United States

All rights reserved. No parts of this publication may be reproduced, stored in a retrieval system, or transmitted in any form or by any means - for example, electronic, photocopy, or recording - without the prior written permission of RestoreFreeSpeech Press. The only exception is brief quotations in printed reviews.

Scripture quotations, unless otherwise indicated, are from the King James Version.

Additional copies of this book, or information on other books can be obtained by visiting:
www.restorefreespeech.org/books

--- About the cover picture ---

The Eye Witness Testimony of Isaac Potts

This story is well documented in the historical records. Isaac Potts, 26 years old, was a resident of Valley Forge, and as a Quaker was opposed to the war. He supervised the grinding of the grain which George Washington ordered the neighboring farmers to bring to his army. The fullest account of Potts' testimony is in the "Diary and Remembrances" of Rev. Nathaniel Randolph Snowden, a Presbyterian minister and a Princeton graduate (Original Manuscript at the Historical Society of Pennsylvania; Call no. PHi.Am.1561-1568).

"I was riding with him (Mr. Potts) near Valley Forge, where the army lay during the war of the Revolution. Mr. Potts was a Senator in our state and a Whig. I told him I was agreeably surprised to find him a friend to his country as the Quakers were mostly Tories. He said, "It was so and I was a rank Tory once, for I never believed that America could proceed against Great Britain whose fleets and armies covered the land and ocean. But something very extraordinary converted me to the good faith."

"What was that?" I inquired. "Do you see that woods, and that plain?" It was about a quarter of a mile from the place we were riding. "There," said he, "laid the army of Washington. It was a most distressing time of ye war, and all were for giving up the ship but that one good man. In that woods," pointing to a close in view, "I heard a plaintive sound, as of a man at prayer. I tied my horse to a sapling and went quietly into the woods and to my astonishment I saw the great George Washington on his knees alone, with his sword on one side and his cocked hat on the other. He was at Prayer to the God of the Armies, beseeching to interpose with his Divine aid, as it was ye Crisis and the cause of the country, of humanity, and of the world.

"Such a prayer I never heard from the lips of man. I left him alone praying. I went home and told my wife, 'I saw a sight and heard today what I never saw or heard before', and just related to her what I had seen and heard and observed. We never thought a man could be a soldier and a Christian, but if there is one in the world, it is Washington. We thought it was the cause of God, and America could prevail."

....

George Washington was not known as a great public speaker, but as he was about to make a speech at the end of the war, he remembered a slip of paper in his pocket and he pulled out his glasses. The crowd went silent when he put his spectacles on as he said, "I see that you notice that I wear glasses. Well, it was to be. I've not only grown old and gray, I've become almost blind in the service of my country." And with that simple, unrehearsed, spontaneous statement, everyone was moved to tears as they had been reminded of who this man was and what he had done for our country.

The respect for Washington was so great that the first proposal for his new title, recommended by John Adams, was, "His Glorious Highness, The President of the United States and Glorious Protector of Our Liberties." Congressman William McClay from Pennsylvania basically said, "What's with Adams? Doesn't he understand what we fought this thing for? It's to get rid of all of that stuff." But this story illustrates the high regard congress had for Washington.

Forward

When one considers the massive amount of work that Roger Anghis has expended to bring this book to the American public.. the question arises .... Why?

What first comes to my mind is the most basic of Christian motives found in John 8:32 "ye shall know the truth and the truth will make you free."

Much to our disadvantage, in our beloved America, has the truth about our founding and our true history been ridiculed, reviled, revised, and then ignored. We are not a better people as a result.

It is my fervent prayer and my sincere hope that Roger's book will have a wide and immediate readership. All those who read it will pass it and its contents on to others.

As a good Christian and patriot, although "his trade" has not been writing, Roger could not and would not sit by and have his faith in CHRIST denied, our country devalued unto judgment and fallen from grace.

When one man stands up he stiffens other men's spines!

Noah Webster one of the founders of American education certainly would applaud your efforts here as he encouraged the teaching of all children Bible and American providential history.

Thank you brother and compatriot Roger, I salute you and I know our posterity will also.

I will have no other king but KING JESUS..Someone has stolen my country (for most certainly I have not given her away) and I want her back now!

Garrett Lear "The Patriot Pastor", Sanbornville, NH

September 6, 2010 AD

Dedicated to Cody, Izabella and Scout to help them learn true American history and the importance of keeping the truth before our eyes at all times.

Bring America Back To Her Religious Roots
By Roger Anghis

Introduction

This book was written after years of talking to people about the strong Christian heritage our forefathers gave us but almost no one was aware of. Our school system has ceased to teach America's true history for almost 75 years. We have three generations of people who know very little about what our Founding Fathers believed, how they believed or how they used their Christian foundation to build the most successful Constitution this world has ever seen.

Many pastors that I have spoken with have no problem with the so-called 'separation of church and state' and have even told me that it was in our Constitution. Because we no longer teach our Constitution in our schools and we, the pastors, do not teach the importance of who we are and where we came

religion by the people. Today's government has turned that around 180° and is now using what used to guarantee freedom of religion to removal of religion from the public square. Even though God has never had a nation without a spiritual leader to influence the political leader, there are many pastors who believe that the church should stay out of politics and believe Christians should not be involved in it either. That teaching is not biblical, nor is it historical in America. This book will open the eyes of most who read it to an America they were not told about. They will learn that our Founding Fathers put their religious beliefs to practice in the building of this great nation. Their religious beliefs were strictly Christian principles and were not confined to their private life but influenced their political lives as well. You find it in their laws, the Declaration of Independence, the Constitution, and the Bill of Rights. You will find it in their personal writings and what they wrote about each other. The Bible was their sole book for morals, government, laws, and society.

religion by the people. Today's government has turned that around 180? and is now using what used to guarantee freedom of religion to removal of religion from the public square. Even though God has never had a nation without a spiritual leader to influence the political leader, there are many pastors who believe that the church should stay out of politics and believe Christians should not be involved in it either. That teaching is not biblical, nor is it historical in America. This book will open the eyes of most who read it to an America they were not told about. They will learn that our Founding Fathers put their religious beliefs to practice in the building of this great nation. Their religious beliefs were strictly Christian principles and were not confined to their private life but influenced their political lives as well. You find it in their laws, the Declaration of Independence, the Constitution, and the Bill of Rights. You will find it in their personal writings and what they wrote about each other. The Bible was their sole book for morals, government, laws, and society.

Many believe that the church was silent during the Revolutionary War but those who taught the people about fair taxation, inalienable rights, the right to own property, choosing the people who are in authority over you and everything else they fought for were the preachers. The British called them the Black Regiment, for the black robes they wore. They were many of the military leaders and many who went to Congress after the war. When the British captured a soldier that they knew was a preacher he was treated harsher than a regular soldier because it was the preacher that kept the fire of revolution going in the hearts of the people.

The church has lost its identity and its purpose concerning the politics of America. They won't preach what God is against for fear of offending someone. When you preach the truth, somebody is going to get offended. Live with it. We must fulfill the mandate that God has given the church as a whole, as our forefathers did, or we will lose the greatest nation this world has ever seen.

I hope that this book inspires you to learn more about the heritage of this great nation. Learn it before it is removed from all of our history books.

Contents

Chapter 1 - The Beginning 2

Chapter 2 - The Foundation 12

Chapter 3 - The Foundation Strengthened 22

Chapter 4 - Original Intent 32

Chapter 5 - The Founders 42

Chapter 6 - Education 52

Chapter 7 - The Documents 60

Chapter 8 - Their Belief 70

Chapter 9 - Their Law 88

Chapter 10 - Their Law (Cont) 78

Chapter 11 - Their Bible 96

Chapter 12 - Their Stand 104

Chapter 13 - The Signs of Apostasy 114

Chapter 14 - The Pastors 122

Chapter 15 - How It Works 130

Chapter 16 - The Practice 140

Chapter 17 - The Fight 150

Chapter 18 - The Finale 158

Prayer For Our Nation 165

Biographies Of The Founding Fathers 167

Chapter 1

The Beginning

Bring America Back To Her Religious Roots

Chapter 1- The Beginning

The religious roots of our nation go very deep. Over the last 50-75 years we have lost a tremendous amount of the truth concerning the history of how Christian religion not only governed the daily lives of our Founding Fathers but how that same faith was always a major factor in the politics of this nation.

In his seminal work, <u>Mein Kampf</u>, Adolf Hitler stated that the bigger the lie and the more often that it is told the easier it is to get the masses to believe it. In the 30's and 40's Hitler did just, that and the result was a world war that cost the lives of over 60 million people.

In 1947 our Supreme Court ruled that the 1st Amendment had erected a "wall of separation" between the church and state, and it had to remain impregnable. There was no preceding evidence of this "truth" in any court ruling for over 170 years, and not even in the first Supreme Court was the church/state position challenged. Yet, the Supreme Court of 1947 decided that our

Bring America Back To Her Religious Roots

Chapter 1 - The Beginning

Founding Fathers were uninformed as to the meaning of the 1st Amendment. The 1947 Supreme Court for the first time used ONLY the phrase "separation of church and state" instead of the whole context of that sentence which is not found in any of our founding documents, but in a letter from Thomas Jefferson to the Danbury Baptist Association in 1802. A letter was written to then President Jefferson because they had a concern that the United States might try to establish a state church as had been done in England. The state ran the church and taxed the people to support the church. When you read the entire letter that Jefferson wrote you will find that he does use the statement "separation of church and state" but it is easily understood that what he is talking about is keeping the government out of the affairs of the church, not keeping the church completely out of the government. In other words the 'separation' was an institutional separation not an influential separation. The Supreme Court decision of 1947 by liberal judges appointed to

Bring America Back To Her Religious Roots

Chapter 1 - The Beginning

the Supreme Court by FDR, completely redefined the 1st Amendment. In that day 97% of the people of this nation declared an allegiance to God and in a nation where the majority rules, the 3% of our nation that did not believe in God ruled over the 97%. In the early 1950's one of the Supreme Court justices warned that we had better STOP using the phrase "separation of church and state" without its proper context or people would begin believing that it was part of our Constitution. Most of the people you and I talk to today, if you ask them about the so-called "separation of church and state" do believe that it is part of our Constitution. The bigger the lie and the more you tell it makes it easier for the masses to believe it.

Preachers today don't believe that the church is supposed to be involved in the political arena and because the church does not address this part of American life we have politicians that won't protect our borders, we have politicians that believe that it is a

Bring America Back To Her Religious Roots

Chapter 1 - The Beginning

woman's *right* to destroy her unborn child and we have politicians that refuse to support our troops fighting the war on terror. The Bible teaches us that however the church goes, the nation goes. Preachers today don't have a problem with how the government has taken our right to be involved in the politics of this nation away from us. Without the church's influence our politicians have begun to take this nation down a path of destruction. And because pastors are afraid of losing their 501(c)3 tax-exempt status, they won't stand up for their rights. I have tried to help pastors educate their people as to what they can and should be doing in terms of their involvement with political issues, and the typical response is, "We don't do anything political". I invited 200 pastors to a meeting concerning this and only one pastor showed up! Some pastors won't even take a side on abortions and same-sex marriages for fear of losing members or their coveted 501(c)3. They claim that it is a political issue. It has become a political issue but

Bring America Back To Her Religious Roots

Chapter 1 - The Beginning

more importantly it is a moral issue that the church should be addressing. Half of the people sitting in the pews are living together without the benefit of marriage but the church won't preach against it for fear of offending someone. One pastor I talked to felt "comfortable" with the American church's present lack of involvement in the political arena. I used to feel the same way until one day the Holy Spirit asked me, 'What if I'm <u>not</u> comfortable with the lack of involvement of the church in the political arena?" That is the question that pastors must ask themselves. Is God happy that the church is absent from the political arena and from the government? There was a point in time in this nation when you couldn't get elected UNLESS you confessed Jesus as Lord and had a record of attending church regularly. Religion was very important during the days of our Founding Fathers. One man was fined $500 for using the Name of the Lord in vain. That was over a year's wages at the time.

Bring America Back To Her Religious Roots

Chapter 1 - The Beginning

Today you hear people inside the church building using language that reminds you of a drunken sailor. I even heard the son of a pastor who could cuss better than some on the streets. Just a short while ago a man in a public meeting cursed and was arrested and jailed. When he got before a judge, the judge told the police that they had violated his right of free speech. What kind of place have we come to in the church and in our nation? Today's churches preach a lukewarm message not wanting to offend anyone. Any time you teach the truth somebody is going to be offended. Lukewarm messages have never built a strong church. **Revelation 3:16** *"So because you are lukewarm, and neither hot nor cold, I will spew you out of My mouth."*

Many of the preachers that I've talked to don't believe that the church is supposed to be involved in the political arena. But in the Bible God ALWAYS had a man or woman of God close to the king, ALWAYS! Saul, Israel's first king had Samuel the

Bring America Back To Her Religious Roots

Chapter 1 - The Beginning

prophet. Every king, whether they were godly or not, had a man of God to influence them. Even our presidents have had godly men to influence them. One man, Billy Graham, has counseled and prayed with every president since Harry Truman. Eleven presidents have been blessed by Dr. Graham's prayers and influence. Every president we have had has had a man of God to advise him and pray for him. Our presidents have not always taken the advice of these godly men just as the kings in the Old Testament didn't always take heed to the advice of the prophets. We have seen some presidents ignore the godly principles of our Founding Fathers and take our nation down a path that leads away from the things of God. One such president was Woodrow Wilson. He was a racist and a progressive with beliefs that were closely akin to Marxism. Later, we had Franklin Delano Roosevelt in the White House. He set this nation on the road to socialism and there are many today in that same political party that are hell-bent on finishing that journey.

Bring America Back To Her Religious Roots

Chapter 1 - The Beginning

They support forcing religious organizations to hire homosexuals. They passed "hate crimes" legislation that could make preaching the Biblical view of homosexuality against the law. Over the years, they have supported the removal of religion from the public view including displays of the Ten Commandment, pictures of Jesus and the removal of prayer from government meetings.

The church has to stand up for its rights or we will lose all of our rights. Many pastors say that we have to abide by the laws. But when the laws of man violate the laws of God, Christians, and especially preachers of the gospel, are required to obey God! When John and Peter were brought before the Sanhedrin and told to no longer speak in the Name of Jesus, Peter refused to follow that order: Acts 4:18 *"And they called them, and commanded them not to speak at all nor teach in the name of Jesus.(19) But Peter and John answered and said unto them, "Whether it be right in the sight of God to hearken unto you*

Bring America Back To Her Religious Roots

Chapter 1 - The Beginning

more than unto God, judge ye".

(20) For we cannot but speak the things which we have seen and heard."

Until 1954 the church leaders could talk about political candidates from the pulpit openly, and whether the individuals and their words and actions were godly or ungodly. We could talk about political parties and whether their platforms and candidates stood for godly things or ungodly things. In 1948, Lyndon Johnson won his first election to the senate by a total of only 87 votes. He had a lot of political connections and was able to stop every attempt at a recount. During the 1954 senatorial campaign, this information was leaked to two 501(c)3 non-profit organizations that then began to inform the public about a possible rigged election. As a result, Johnson had language inserted into the IRS codes that barred any 501(c)3 from supporting or opposing a political candidate or a political party. Johnson was able to silence his opposition. The church had been silenced ever since.

Chapter 2

The Foundation

Bring America Back To Her Religious Roots

Chapter 2 – The Foundation

The 1st Amendment states: "Congress shall make no law respecting the establishment of religion, or prohibiting the free exercise thereof." This Amendment has been violated for years. We will discuss this in this chapter.

The church's responsibility is to inform the public as to the qualifications required of our leaders. In Exodus 18:21, God spoke to Moses through the wise counsel of his father-in-law, Jethro, saying, *"Moreover thou shalt provide out of all the people able men, such as fear God, men of truth, hating covetousness; and place such over them, to be rulers of thousands, and rulers of hundreds, rulers of fifties, and rulers of tens:"*. These "rulers" were to settle minor disputes themselves, but would bring major issues to Moses for final judgment. Those men became the government of the nation of Israel.

Until 1954 we could "name names" and compare candidates or office holders to each other and to Biblical standards. Now we

Bring America Back To Her Religious Roots

Chapter 2 - The Foundation

can only generalize. The changes to the IRS tax codes that Congress passed in 1954 prohibited the church from informing the people of the character of a political candidate. That change to tax laws prohibited the free exercise of religion and directly violates the 1st Amendment to the Constitution of the United States. Public schools were originally established and funded by tax dollars so that the people would be taught to read and understand the Word of God with the Bible being its main source for information. We will discuss this more in Chapter 6. If government tried to pass legislation that was contrary to God's Word the people would know it and then take action to stop it. We have allowed our government to redefine our Constitution and read things into it that our Founding Fathers would never have allowed. We have allowed activist judges to read into our Constitution the "right to privacy" by which a woman can obtain an abortion at any time for any reason. To fully understand just what the role of the church is supposed to

Bring America Back To Her Religious Roots

Chapter 2 - The Foundation

be in this nation we have to look at the role of the church before our independence, during our fight for independence and up until 1954 when the church was taken out of the political arena. Many of you will be surprised to learn how deeply involved the church and the Word of God was in the drafting of our Declaration of Independence, our Constitution, and the Bill of Rights. I know that there will be many pastors that will be shocked at the church's involvement in the development of our government. Too many pastors believe that the church shouldn't be involved in politics at all. What this book will reveal will be unfamiliar to many pulpits. Revisionist historians have taught what THEY want you to believe instead of what the real history actually is.

There was a book printed that contained the writings of George Washington on four different areas of life. The original book contained comments by his contemporaries. The book is now being printed again. However, the comments are now by

Bring America Back To Her Religious Roots

Chapter 2 - The Foundation

Revisionists and they have left out almost all of the religious references from the original book and all of the commentaries of his contemporaries and the revisionists commentaries refer to him as a deist. How you can print a book that is full of outright lies and call it historically accurate is beyond me.

Our Founding Fathers took their faith very seriously but many today would like you to believe differently. When the Massachusetts Bay colony was established in 1620, the "pilgrims" established why they were there before they got off of the boat. They wrote the Mayflower Compact.

"In the Name of God, Amen. We, whose names are underwritten, the loyal subjects of our Sovereign Lord, King James, by the Grace of God, or England, France and Ireland, King defender of the Faith,Having undertaken for the Glory of God, and <u>Advancement of the Christian Faith</u>, and the Honor of our King and Country, a voyage to plant the first colony in the

Bring America Back To Her Religious Roots

Chapter 2 - The Foundation

northern parts of Virginia; do by these presents, solemnly and mutually in the Presence of God and one of another, covenant and combine ourselves together into a civil Body Politick, for our better Ordering and Preservation, and Furtherance of the Ends aforesaid;"

The "Ends aforesaid" was **the advancement of the Christian faith**. Our Founding Fathers lived their faith. Most churches today have a 30 minute message ending with "Call our office Monday-Friday between 9-5 if you want to get saved." Most modern Americans couldn't handle the church services in those days. They usually lasted from 4-6 hours and most of the town would attend. It was a firm belief of our Founding Fathers that to serve in public office you had to be a Christian.

We generally understand and agree that the primary purpose and function of the United States Supreme Court is to decide if the laws that are passed by Congress fall within the parameters set out by the Constitution. John Jay, the first Chief Justice of the

Bring America Back To Her Religious Roots

Chapter 2 - The Foundation

Supreme Court stated, *"Providence has given our people the choice of their rulers. It is the duty as well as the privilege and the interest **of our Christian nation** to select and prefer Christians as their rulers."*

Another of our Founding Fathers was Patrick Henry. His most famous (shortened) statement was "Give me liberty or give me death." This is not being taught in schools any more. It promotes patriotism and self-worth and that causes problems with dictating what some people want you to believe. Another statement attributed to him, which I assure you will never be taught in public schools is this one: *"It can't be emphasized too strongly or too often that this great nation was founded NOT by religionists, but by Christians; not on religion but on the gospel of Jesus Christ."* The revisionist historians want you to believe that Patrick Henry was a deist. (A deist generally believes a supreme being created the universe and that this truth can be known without either faith or organized religion. In most cases,

Bring America Back To Her Religious Roots

Chapter 2 - The Foundation

a deist also rejects the idea that God intervenes in human affairs.) The revisionists want you to believe that most of the Founding Fathers were deists, even though ALL evidence proves otherwise. People simply don't research anything out for themselves. There were 55 signers of the Constitution- 29 were Episcopalians, several were Methodist, and some were Baptist and 32 held seminary degrees. There was only one alleged deist and that was Ben Franklin, but even he had enough sense to know that Providence should be called upon at times. Members of the Constitutional Convention had spent weeks debating key provisions of the Constitution without making any progress. During that time of intense debate, Franklin addressed the Convention on June 28, 1787. A part of that speech reads, *"All of us who were engaged in this struggle must have observed frequent instances of superintending Providence in our favor."* So, that statement by BenFranklin effectively destroys the revisionist's theory about him. The next few

Bring America Back To Her Religious Roots

Chapter 2 - The Foundation

sentences of his speech "seals the deal" on refuting his so-called deism: *"To that kind Providence we owe this happy opportunity of consulting, in peace, on the means of establishing our future national felicity. And have we now forgotten that powerful Friend, or do we imagine that we no longer need His assistance? I have lived, Sir, a long time and the longer I live the more convincing proofs I see this truth, that God governs the affairs of men. And if a sparrow cannot fall to the ground without His notice, is it probable that an empire can rise without His aid?"*

Following that speech, our Founding Fathers spent four hours in prayer. In a public facility, our government officials had prayer and then followed that with preaching - the message was so moving that John Adams wrote to his wife about how important it was. From that moment on the Constitution began to come together with surprising ease.

Thirteen years earlier, Samuel Adams, a signer of the Declaration of Independence who would become the governor

Bring America Back To Her Religious Roots

Chapter 2 - The Foundation

of Massachusetts, wrote; *"We have this day restored the Sovereign to whom all men ought to be obedient, He reigns in heaven from the rising to the setting of the sun. Let His kingdom come."* He also made this statement: *"Pray that the light of the gospel and the right of conscience may be continued to the people of the United America and that His Holy Word may be improved by them so that the Name of God will be exalted and their liberty and happiness be secure. That He would be pleased to bless our federal government."* The Foundation is laid.

Chapter 3

The Foundation Strengthened

Bring America Back To Her Religious Roots

Chapter 3 – The Foundation Strengthened

I mention several quotes from our Founding Fathers because there are those who have tried to deceive the younger generations to believe that our Founding Fathers were not practicing Christians and that the United States was NOT founded as a Christian nation. Our Founders believed in the power of the Word of God and they lived their lives accordingly. Using their own words is the best way to understand their belief.

We have seen this nation turn against its founding principles to the point where once the Bible was the only book used in school to just recently a child was ARRESTED for reading their Bible during study hall. Christmas plays can't have Christmas carols or even the mention of Christmas because it is a religious holiday and we must maintain the so-called "separation of church and state".

Halloween, which roots are in Satanism, is accepted and

Bring America Back To Her Religious Roots
Chapter 3 - The Foundation Strengthened

celebrated in our schools. Even though Satanism is recognized as a religion, there is no demand to stop this celebration. What we are seeing is an outright attack only on Christianity and Judaism. Islam is being taught in some California schools and in some Michigan schools. They are even having them pray to Allah in these schools, but you can't have a picture of Jesus hanging in these same schools. Revisionist historians refuse to write what the contemporaries said about our Founders because it conflicts with what *they* want you to believe. We have at least two generations of children that have been refused the truth about the role of Christianity in the building of our nation and our government.

We must learn again the role of the church in our government and our daily affairs. Paul gives us instructions on the matter in 1 Timothy 2:1 *"I exhort therefore, that, first of all, supplications, prayers, intercessions, and giving of thanks, be made for all men;*

Bring America Back To Her Religious Roots

Chapter 3 - The Foundation Strengthened

(2) For kings, and for all that are in authority; that we may lead a quiet and peaceable life in all godliness and honesty.
(3) For this is good and acceptable in the sight of God our Savior". It is foolishness to elect ungodly people and then pray that they act godly. To think that the church/Christians/ should not be involved in the political arena is not even a Biblical viewpoint. When I was growing up I was taught that a Christian doesn't get involved in politics because it is so corrupt. But that is the very reason Christians SHOULD be in politics, to bring respect to that office. We have had a recent president bring disgrace to the office of the president and he was followed by a president who brought respect and dignity back to the office of the president. Romans 13:3 *"For rulers are not a terror to good works, but to the evil. Wilt thou then not be afraid of the power? Do that which is good, and thou shalt have praise of the same:"*
It is the duty of the church to see to it that godly men and

Bring America Back To Her Religious Roots

Chapter 3 - The Foundation Strengthened

women govern this nation. John Adams states this about our government: *"We have no government armed with power capable of contending with human passions unbridled by morality and religion. . . . Our Constitution was made only for a moral and religious people. It is wholly inadequate to the government of any other."*

Today's historians are more fiction writers than true historians and they claim that most of the Founding Fathers were atheists, agnostics, and deists. They claim that none were Christians and that none of our Founding Documents had any religious references. One Supreme Court justice has even stated that Thomas Jefferson wrote the First Amendment to keep religion out of government. The biggest problem with that statement is that Thomas Jefferson was in France when the First Amendment was written and he never even saw it until after it was ratified. Fisher Ames was the author of the First Amendment. Congressional records show that on September

Bring America Back To Her Religious Roots

Chapter 3 - The Foundation Strengthened

17, 1787 the wording for the First Amendment was agreed upon and that Ames was the author. Another problem with that statement is it was not written to keep religion out of government but to keep government out of religion. If Jefferson really did believe that religion and government required an "impregnable" wall of separation, as the Supreme Court stated, then why, when he was President, were ALL government buildings in Washington open for the purpose of holding church services in them and the military band was made available for praise and worship? One has to wonder why when the 10 Commandments are carved into the stone walls of the Supreme Court that the same Court has declared that displays of the 10 Commandments are unconstitutional in other courthouses. The history of America that has been taught to the last 2-3 generations is more lie than truth. The history that they are teaching did NOT occur, for the most part, and the real history is not allowed to be told. I want to establish with you the true

Bring America Back To Her Religious Roots

Chapter 3 - The Foundation Strengthened

beliefs of our Founding Fathers and not my opinion or someone else's opinion, but their own words concerning what they believed. Zephaniah Swift was an American jurist in Connecticut and served in the House of Representatives. He was also the first Chief Justice of Connecticut's Supreme Court and declared that Christianity was THE guiding influence on everyday living in his day: *"Indeed moral virtue is substantially and essentially enforced by the precepts of Christianity and may be considered the basis of it. But in addition to moral principles the Christian doctrines inculcate a purity of heart and holiness of life that constitutes its chief glory. When we contemplate it in this light, we have a most striking evidence of its superiority over all the systems of pagan philosophy, which were promulgated by the wisest men of ancient times."*

When looking at the reasons for the establishment of each of our colonies it becomes very clear that the establishing of

Bring America Back To Her Religious Roots

Chapter 3 - The Foundation Strengthened

Christianity and evangelizing the region teaching the natives about Christianity was the purpose of the colony. All 13 colonies were established for this purpose. In 1606 the charter for the colony of Virginia stated, *"To make habitations and to deduce a colony of sundry of our people into that part of American commonly called Virginia in **propagating the Christian religion to such people as yet live in darkness**."*
(Emphasis added)

William Bradford who helped compose the Mayflower Compact, stated the purpose of why the Pilgrims had come to the New World: *". . . a great hope and inward zeal they had of laying some good foundation, or at least to make some way thereunto, **for the propagating and advancing the Gospel of the kingdom of Christ** in those remote parts of the world."*
(Emphasis added)

A decade later the Puritans began to arrive and one of their great leaders John Winthrop, warned them of the consequences of

Bring America Back To Her Religious Roots

Chapter 3 - The Foundation Strengthened

forgetting their goal: *"We are a company professing ourselves fellow-members of Christ . . . knit together by this bond of love . . . We are entered into a covenant with Him for this work. . . For we must consider that we shall be as a city upon a hill, the eyes of all people are upon us; so that if we shall deal falsely with our God in this work we have undertaken and so cause Him to withdraw His present help from us, well shall be made a story and a byword through the world."* Does this sound like the policy of a secularist nation? The Foundation is strengthened.

Chapter 4

Original Intent

Bring America Back To Her Religious Roots

Chapter 4 – Original Intent

In looking at the charters for the colonies we see that establishing Christianity was the main purpose for their developing the colony.

The 1629 charter of Massachusetts states: "*Our said people be so religiously, peaceably, and civilly governed that their good life and orderly conversation may win and incite the natives of that country to the knowledge and obedience of the one true God and savior of mankind, and the Christian faith, which is the principle end of this colony.*"

The 1662 charter for North Carolina stated that they were: "*Excited with a laudable and pious zeal for **the propagation of the Christian faith** in the parts of American not yet cultivated or planted and only inhabited by people who have no knowledge of Almighty God.*" (Emphasis added) This, again, is not the policy of a secular nation.

In 1663 the charter for Rhode Island explained the colonist's

Bring America Back To Her Religious Roots

Chapter 4 - Original Intent

intent: *"Pursuing with Peace and loyal minds, their sober, serious and religious intentions of Godly edifying themselves and one another in the holy Christian faith, a most flourishing civil state may stand and best be maintained with a full liberty in religious concernments."* Does this sound like the policy of a secular nation?

William Penn wrote the charter for Pennsylvania stating: *"Out of a commendable desire to **convert the savage natives by gentle and just manners to the love of civil society and Christian religion**, hath humbly besought leave of us to transport an ample colony unto a certain country in the parts of America not yet cultivated or planted."* (Emphasis Added)

The charter of Connecticut, New Hampshire, New Jersey and others were a virtual restatement of the Christian goals stated by these states. Connecticut had the first constitution and in 1639 it stated: *"Well knowing when a people are gathered together, the Word of God requires that to maintain the peace and union of*

Bring America Back To Her Religious Roots

Chapter 4 - Original Intent

such people there should be an orderly and decent government established according to God." Secular people do NOT establish government according to God (Russia, China and Cuba as examples). Their constitution went on to declare the colonists desire to: *"Enter into combination and confederation together to maintain and preserve the liberty and purity of the Gospel of our Lord Jesus which we now profess which, according to the truth of the said Gospel, is now practiced amongst us."* If they were not Christians why would they put in writing that they were?

To ignore what our Founding Fathers wrote and to declare that our Founding Fathers were not Christian is nothing less than foolish not to mention deceptive. We all know that our enemy is a master at deception. He's a liar, a thief and a murderer. Jesus stated in John 8:44, *"Ye are of your father the devil, and the lusts of your father ye will do. He was a murderer from the beginning, and abode not in the truth, because there is no truth*

Bring America Back To Her Religious Roots

Chapter 4 - Original Intent

in him. When he speaketh a lie, he speaketh of his own: for he is a liar, and the father of it". How do we know if the devil is lying? His lips are moving. Our enemy does not want this younger generation to know that it was Christianity that made America the great nation that it is today. If they find out that Christianity is what made this nation great, there is a good chance that many will pursue Christianity and he will not make the progress that he wants to make. We have allowed liberal Presidents, members of Congress and judges to redefine our Constitution and Bill of rights to fit their socialist agenda. There are members of congress that are doing everything they can to shut the church up and remove its influence in government.

In 1954 Lyndon Johnson was able to partially shut the church up. Ted Kennedy tried and others are trying to silence the church even more with the passing of the so-called "hate crimes" bill where it could be illegal to even read the biblical

Bring America Back To Her Religious Roots

Chapter 4 - Original Intent

point of view about homosexuality. This legislation is now in effect and there are "hate crime"' lawsuits against students for putting a Bible on a teacher's desk. Some preachers are now getting liability insurance so they can have a buffer against any possible litigation. When our leaders ignore the Word of God the laws of this nation will reflect that. Even legislators that are professed Christians demand abortion upon demand, support same-sex marriage, and support the hate crimes bill.

Here are some statistics about the apathy in the church today. Of our population today 83% claim to be Christian. Of that figure 46% are protestant and attend weekly with 56% in the south. In 2006 a poll was taken and out of this group of Christians only 11% felt that abortion should be banned. 35% want it legal in rare instances. Abortion has always been available when the life of the mother is at stake. Planned Parenthood says that abortion is a health issue. Over 90% of abortions are done for convenience, not health. When asked if

Bring America Back To Her Religious Roots

Chapter 4 - Original Intent

there should be state laws that would allow terminally ill patients to end their lives 52% said yes. 58% stated that it wouldn't be a problem if their child's elementary teacher was a homosexual. (100% of the male teachers that attack male students are homosexual.) 45% would allow their child to read a book about a same-sex couples. 42% of adults between the ages of 18 and 44 approve of homosexual rights. Over all Americans are split 42% to 42% as to whether they approve of homosexual rights. 70% of Americans do not believe that the military should have the right to discharge someone who lives the gay lifestyle. Who wants to be on the battlefield with someone who might have AIDS and could contaminate others if they get shot? 62% feel that homosexuals should have the same rights that racial minorities and women have. 50% of Americans support some form of legal status for same-sex couples.

Would we see these kinds of statistics in the colonies? I don't

Bring America Back To Her Religious Roots

Chapter 4 - Original Intent

think so. They would spend on average 4 hours a day studying the Word of God and they knew and believed God's commandments. Most Christians today don't spend 4 hours a month in the Word. In 1643 Massachusetts, Connecticut, New Plymouth and New Haven joined together to form the New England Confederation which was Americas first united government. They banded together because they all had the same goal: *"We all came into these parts of America with one and the same end and aim, namely **to advance the kingdom of our Lord Jesus Christ.**"* (Emphasis Added)

In 1669, John Locke assisted in the drafting of the Carolina constitution under which no man could be a citizen unless he acknowledged God, was a member of a church, and used no reproachful, reviling, or abusive language against any religion. Can you imagine if that was still a requirement in any state constitution today? If you were not a believer in the state of Connecticut you were not allowed to even camp in that state.

Bring America Back To Her Religious Roots

Chapter 4 - Original Intent

They didn't want you there for any reason. These documents are proof that Christianity was the prominent influence in the early growth and development of our civil government.

Chapter 5

The Founders

Bring America Back To Her Religious Roots

Chapter 5 – The Founders

We have to go back in the lives of those who came to this country to understand why they came to America. What was their motivation to leave everything in Europe or England and risk it all to come to America? Let us look at what caused these people to come here. Most came with very little possessions. Most had to sell all they had to make the trip. But all came with one thing in common, a Bible. It was usually the Geneva Bible. This Bible was not popular in England because there were commentaries in it by people that were referred to as dissenters; Calvin, Martin Luther. You also have to keep in mind that this was the first time in history were the common person had a copy of the Bible. In the late 1600's and early 1700's in Europe only clergy were permitted to even read the Bible. It was illegal for the common person to read the Bible. A lot of the religious persecution in those days was because the common people would read the Bible and see where the king was not following

Bring America Back To Her Religious Roots

Chapter 5 - The Founders

the Word of God and they would complain. The biggest area of friction was when the common person found out that God didn't want Israel to have an earthly king. The people decided that they wanted a government as God declared, kingless. This didn't set well with royalty. This is where we see why Thomas Jefferson called for the separation of church and state. Again that was to keep government **out** of religion. It was an institutional separation not an influential separation. In England, there was only one authorized version of scripture that was allowed. All other versions were illegal. The king declared what you teach and how you teach it. This is why Jefferson stated that the "wall of separation" was to keep government out of religion, not religion out of government. Remember, Jefferson did not write the First Amendment, Fisher Ames did. The concern of government intervention in the church was the reason for the letter from the Danbury Baptist association to Thomas Jefferson. They were concerned that what had

Bring America Back To Her Religious Roots

Chapter 5 - The Founders

happened in England with the Church of England would happen in America.

As the common person began to read the Bible they began to see that not everything that the church was teaching was biblical. We can even see this today in the church with some denominations teaching that homosexuality is OK, abortion is OK, and the church is not to be involved in the political arena. According to IRS regulations we are not allowed to endorse a political party or candidate nor are we allowed to speak against a political party or candidate. Those are IRS regulations, not God's. The church has more of a reverential fear of the IRS than they do of God. The most prominent sermon throughout America's history was the one given around elections talking about the importance of the church's role in the political arena, specifically the presidential election. Today's laws over the church restrict what I can and cannot say about candidates and their party. This is a violation of my First Amendment right to

Bring America Back To Her Religious Roots

Chapter 5 - The Founders

freedom of speech and freedom of religion and the free exercise thereof. As a pastor I am mandated to inform my congregation of ungodly men and women who are running for office. Oddly enough, there is a legal way around that restriction that most churches ignore. They just find it easier to not get involved at all. That is why our nation is in the shape that it is in.

I believe that the ignorance of the pastors is more damaging to our nation that the ignorance of the people themselves concerning what our rights are. Almost everyone that I have asked the question concerning the separation of the church and state has told me that it is in our Constitution. It is not in ANY of our Founding Documents and the First Amendment has been grossly misinterpreted since 1947 by liberal judges that were allowed to redefine its meaning and purpose. Our history refutes any notion that the church is supposed to be removed from the political arena. In the 1947 Supreme Court decision the letter to Jefferson from the Danbury Baptist Association was

Bring America Back To Her Religious Roots

Chapter 5 - The Founders

quoted but only the nine words "building a wall of separation between church and state." This is the first time the Supreme Court used only those nine words. This letter had been used is several other cases before the Supreme Court but the entire contents were used, not just those nine words. When taken out of context the true meaning is lost which is why the Supreme Court did it in that manner. To understand this let's look at a larger portion of that 1802 letter that gives a better understanding of its contents and meaning. Jefferson wrote:

"Believing with you that religion is a matter which lies solely between man and his God; that he owes account to none for his faith and his worship; that the legislative powers of government reach actions only and not opinions, I contemplate with sovereign reverence that act of the whole American people which declared that their legislature should "make no law respecting an establishment of religion of prohibiting the free exercise thereof," thus building a wall of separation between

Bring America Back To Her Religious Roots

Chapter 5 - The Founders

church and state." This clearly indicates that the government is to stay out of religion and gives no indication that religion is to stay out of government. Today there are organizations that are ignorant of scripture and the history of the United States. There is even one organization, Americans United for the Separation of Church and State, which is headed by a so-called reverend. He is grossly misinformed as to what the church is supposed to be doing in the political arena not to mention his ignorance of the history of the church in this nation and the real meaning of the Constitution.

One of the things that the people began to realize when they started to read the Bible is how to apply the Word of God in everyday lives such as morals, righteousness, forgiveness and all that God has called the church to be. We were to be self governed, not ruled over by an earthly king. They also realized that the church is supposed to evangelize. That is why we see in virtually every charter of every colony a provision that calls for

Bring America Back To Her Religious Roots

Chapter 5 - The Founders

that colony to reach out to the native population with the knowledge of Jesus Christ. . It started with the Mayflower Compact, a call to evangelize. This was something that the king did not allow. It was even illegal to print a Bible in the colonies until after the Revolutionary War. They could only use the "approved" version supplied by England. They discovered in the Word of God that we were supposed to own our own property. The pilgrims began to buy land from the Indians and divide it up amongst the families. This didn't set well with the king. He felt that he owned the land and we were to use it and he would take all the profits and let us keep barely enough to get by on and then he would tax you on that. Kind of sounds like the IRS today doesn't it? The Founders discovered in the Word of God that we were to take care of our own. They also discovered that if you won't work you don't eat. When Jamestown was founded they operated on what would be called today a socialistic form of government. But when looked at real

Bring America Back To Her Religious Roots

Chapter 5 - The Founders

close it was a Biblical system where everybody's needs were addressed by the people, NOT a forced redistribution of your goods by the government as we see our government trying to do today.

When it came to education, Europe had a high percentage of illiteracy and the people in America began to see that the atrocities that had happened in the world happened because of ignorance of the Word of God. In America they began to teach children how to read and write so that everyone would be able to know when government was attempting to do something that was contrary to the Word of God. Their textbook was the Bible. The first schools were run by the church. This was the foundation our Founding Fathers were established in.

Chapter 6

Education

Bring America Back To Her Religious Roots

Chapter 6 – Education

To understand how important education was to the colonists and how they treated it we have to go back to the middle of the 17th century. From this we see America treating education like no other nation previously had done before. It was something that the colonists believed was vital to a moral society.

The first laws providing public education for all children were passed in 1642 in Massachusetts and in 1647 in Connecticut and it was called the "Old Deluder Satan Law". These colonists believed that the proper protection from civil abuses could only be achieved by eliminating Bible illiteracy. This way the people themselves, as opposed to only the leaders, could measure the acts of civil government compared to the teachings of scripture. By 1690 Connecticut had a law that required that children be educated and if the children were not being educated the family would be fined $25.00. Their reasoning here was that if a person can't read then they will not be aware of what God's

Bring America Back To Her Religious Roots
Chapter 6 – Education

laws are and they would not be able to know when the government was trying to do something that was contrary to the Word of God. This shows that it wasn't important to just be able to read, but to read and understand the Word of God. If only our education system was like this today. Today a teacher can't even have a Bible IN their desk. You can't post the Ten Commandments in a classroom because someone might read them and obey them. God forbid that a student obey the Ten Commandments. How many teen pregnancies would we have if the children obeyed the Ten Commandments? How many school shootings would we have if the students obeyed the Ten Commandments? How many students would be on drugs and alcohol if they obeyed the Ten Commandments? The church in the days of our Founding fathers was not a social club like it is today. They understood the importance of living a Christian life. Too many of our preachers today do not teach that importance. Our Founding Fathers' Christianity was a way of

Bring America Back To Her Religious Roots

Chapter 6 - Education

life and they expected those that governed them to live the same way. There were a couple of states that would not allow you to run for political office unless you attended a church and had confessed Jesus Christ as Lord. Try that today and you'll end up in court with five different organizations suing you. Say a prayer in school and the same thing will happen. Our rights and privileges as Christians have been taken away from us little by little. I believe that it is the fault of the pastors refusing to stand for what is right. Refusing to stand for what our Founding Fathers fought and died for, risked all for. Will we just sit back and do nothing or will we stand together and say "No more"? As for me and my house we will serve the Lord.

They believed that everyone should be able to read so that our government officials could not pass laws that were contrary to God's Word. Today the public is better educated than any generation before us, but we still allow laws to be passed that are contrary to God's Word. And that is because we do not

Bring America Back To Her Religious Roots

Chapter 6 - Education

know the Word of God.

When the pilgrims came to America they brought with them text books but in 1690 the first American textbook was printed. It was called the New England Primer. This textbook was the beginning textbook for **ALL** students in America from 1690 to the early 1900's in public, private, semiprivate, home, parochial and all other types of schooling. All of our Founding Fathers learned how to read using the New England Primer and the Bible. Over the 200+ years that it was used, there were very few changes made to the book. This book did not change in that 200+ years period of time except more reading and vocabulary words were added but the core of the Primer - its rhyming alphabet, the Bible alphabet, its Bible questions and Shorter Catechism remained intact from reprint to reprint. This book was so important to our Founding Fathers that they endorsed this book and had it reprinted so that their children would be educated with the same book. Noah Webster who wrote part of

Bring America Back To Her Religious Roots

Chapter 6 - Education

the Constitution, Benjamin Franklin, signer of the Declaration of Independence and the Constitution, Samuel Adams, the Father of the American Revolution, were all responsible for reprints of the New England Primer so it would be available to their children in their generation. When our nation attained freedom from Britain we can see all of the Biblical teachings come into play in the developing of our Constitution and the laws of our land. The Declaration of Independence is the most successful document in the world. No other nation has been governed by a document longer than we have by the Declaration of Independence. Political scientists tell us that our Constitution was based on the same book that was used to write the Declaration of Independence and that book was The Two Treatises of Civil Government by John Locke. The revisionist historians of today say that he was a deist, but he was actually a theologian. He wrote the first topical Bible. He did a book on a verse by verse study of the Bible. He wrote a book titled "The

Bring America Back To Her Religious Roots

Chapter 6 - Education

Reasonableness of Christianity" and he helped write the constitution of Carolina. John Locke's book, The Two Treatises of Civil Government, was the basis for the most successful government document ever written, the Constitution of the United States. Is it any wonder that our government has been the most successful in the world?

John Adams - *"The general principles for which we achieved independence are the general principles of Christianity."*

After we won our independence we began to print Bibles, something that we were not allowed to do while under the rule of Britain. The British government told us what Bible we could use and what could be taught and how it would be taught. This is why the government was to stay out of the church. The very first act of Congress was a 4 hour prayer meeting followed by a sermon that John Adams mentioned to his wife, Abigail, as to how moving it was for him and other members of Congress. One of the other items that Congress did was apportion money

Bring America Back To Her Religious Roots

Chapter 6 - Education

for the printing of Bibles. The record of Congress states that this printing will be "**A meet addition to the Holy Scriptures for use in our public schools.**" This was a printing of the Bible under the supervision of Congress for use in our public schools. This statement was printed on the inside cover of that Bible: "Resolved that the United States and Congress assembled recommend this edition of the Bible to the inhabitants of the United States." Today the ACLU and others declare that our Founding Fathers demanded separation of church and state. This refutes ALL of their arguments.

Education was deemed very important to the colonists and our Founding Fathers but it was all based on the need to understand the Word of God. Today we educate without the benefit of the Word of God and we are experiencing the folly of omitting the foundation for knowledge. It is time we re-think how we attempt to gain knowledge.

Chapter 7

The Documents

Bring America Back To Her Religious Roots

Chapter 7 – The Documents

What we have seen so far has been a total dedication to Christianity by our Founding Fathers AND the majority of the population of America. Revisionists have demanded that a new history be told that never happened. Because of their hatred for, not just religion, but Christianity in particular, we have seen our nation go from God lovers to God haters. They have no problem with our children dressing up on Halloween, a high holy day in Satanism, they have no problem with our children saying prayers to Allah in our public schools, but our schools can't even have a picture of Jesus hanging in the hallway. We can't say a pray at graduation or at a sporting event. We can't sing Christmas carols at Christmas programs and in many states we can't even call Christmas, Christmas.

Some of the court rulings in recent years show the bias of our liberal judges. **Court Ruling:** Freedom of speech is guaranteed to students and teachers *unless* it is religion at which time such speech becomes unconstitutional. **Court Ruling:** It is

Bring America Back To Her Religious Roots

Chapter 7 - The Documents

unconstitutional for students to see the Ten Commandments as they may read them, meditate on them, respect them and obey them. **Court Ruling:** The Ten Commandments, despite the fact that they are the basis of our civil law, and depicted in engraved stone in the Supreme Court building on the wall behind the seats of the justices of the Supreme Court and on the Back of the doors in the Court Chamber, it is against the law to display the Ten Commandments in any government building. **Court Ruling:** It is unconstitutional for any school library to contain books on Christianity. Books on witchcraft are OK. Books on occults are OK. Books on Islam are OK or Buddhism or Hinduism are OK. It is unconstitutional for a teacher to have a copy of the Bible IN his/her desk. Not on it, but in it. **Court Ruling:** It is unconstitutional for school officials to be praised publicly or to be recognized from a podium at a community meeting IF the meeting is sponsored by a religious organization. Planned Parenthood can do that, but a Christian organization

Bring America Back To Her Religious Roots

Chapter 7 - The Documents

cannot do that. **Court Ruling:** It is unconstitutional for a Kindergarten class to ask Who's birthday is celebrated at Christmas. A student in Illinois was arrested, threatened with mace and handcuffed and removed from the school for participating in the See You At The Pole prayer event. In Texas a student was warned that if she prayed she would be disciplined the same as if she had used profanity. A group of individuals were threatened with arrest and prosecution by the US Capitol police for bowing their heads during a silent prayer. The influence of the Bible was so instilled into the hearts and the minds of the Founding Fathers as well as the people that it is no wonder that when drafting the Constitution we find its influence all through the document. An independent study was done by the University of Houston and they wanted to determine what was the biggest influence in drafting the Constitution. They gathered documents from the founding era, 1760-1805, documents that led to the establishing of our

Bring America Back To Her Religious Roots

Chapter 7 - The Documents

Declaration of Independence and what gave us our Constitution. They wanted to see who our Founding Fathers read, quoted and who they were influenced by.

They collected 15,000 documents and from those documents they found 3,154 quotes. It took them 10 years to document these quotes as to where they came from and they discovered that the most quoted source was quoted four times more than the second most quoted source. The most quoted source was the Bible. Established in the original writings of our Founding Fathers we find that they discovered in Isaiah 33:22 the three branches of government: Isaiah 33:22 *"For the LORD is our judge, the LORD is our lawgiver, the LORD is our king; he will save us."* Here we see the judicial, the legislative and the executive branches. In Ezra 7:24 we see where they established the tax exempt status of the church: Ezra 7:24 *"Also we certify you, that touching any of the priests and Levites, singers, porters, Nethinims, or ministers of this house of God, **it***

Bring America Back To Her Religious Roots

Chapter 7 - The Documents

shall not be lawful to impose toll, tribute, or custom*, upon them."*

When we look at our Constitution we see in Article 4 Section 4 that we are guaranteed a Republican form of government, that was found in Exodus 18:21: *"Moreover thou **shalt provide out of all the people able men**, such as fear God, men of truth, hating covetousness; and place such over them, to be rulers of thousands, and rulers of hundreds, rulers of fifties, and rulers of tens:"* This indicates that we are to choose, or elect God fearing men and women. Looking at Article 3 Section 3 we see almost word for word Deuteronomy 17:6: 'No person shall be convicted of Treason unless on the testimony of two Witnesses. . .' Deuteronomy 17:6 *"At the mouth of two witnesses, or three witnesses. . ."*. The next paragraph in Article 3 Section 3 refers to who should pay the price for treason. In England they could punish the sons for the trespasses of the father if the father died. Our Constitution states that only the one guilty of the crime

Bring America Back To Her Religious Roots
Chapter 7 - The Documents

pays for the crime. In 1791 Benjamin Rush, who served for 3 different Presidents, John Adams, Thomas Jefferson, James Madison and was a signer of the Declaration of Independence, started the Sunday School movement in America to deal with the uneducated in the inner cities. It was this same year that Benjamin Rush proposed the idea of public schools. He is actually called the Father of Public Schools in America. If public schools were intended to be the godless institutions that they are today his writings should exhibit that philosophy. What he does say is far from that idea. He believed that the Bible should be the primary book of learning in the public school. He stated: *"Without religion, learning does real mischief to the morals and principles of mankind."* His reference to 'religion' was not any religion, but Christianity exclusively. We have to remember that in the days of our Founding Fathers, their reference to 'religion' was not a generic reference as we see today meaning Christian, Buddhist, Hindu,

Bring America Back To Her Religious Roots

Chapter 7 - The Documents

etc. If they asked what religion you were, they were referring to Baptist, Episcopalian, Methodist, etc. They almost never considered anything other than Christianity. Benjamin Rush believed that you had to teach the Ten Commandments, the Beatitudes, and the morals that are found in the Bible, because he believed, and rightfully so, that to educate without that type of foundation would produce a self centered person that was only concerned about himself. Where did he get that concept? **Proverbs 4:7** *"Wisdom is the principal thing; therefore get wisdom: and with all thy getting get understanding."* **Proverbs 14:8** *"The wisdom of the prudent is to understand his way: but the folly of fools is deceit."* Wisdom is the ability to correctly use the knowledge that you have. Our colleges today fill you with knowledge, but without wisdom all of that knowledge is useless. How else can a student spend 10 years in school learning to be a doctor and then spend his career performing abortions? How else can a student spend years in school

Bring America Back To Her Religious Roots

Chapter 7 - The Documents

learning history, yet not understanding the history he learned? Benjamin Rush was the author of a paper that was literally distributed all across the nation for years, even after his death that was titled "The Use of the Bible In Schools". In that paper he stated, *"If they were ever to take the Bible out of public schools, we would be spending all of our time and all of our money fighting crime when it could be prevented in the classroom."* We are there.

Chapter 8

Their Belief

Bring America Back To Her Religious Roots

Chapter 8 – Their Belief

In the last segment we ended with a quote from Benjamin Rush: *"If they were ever to take the Bible out of public schools, we would be spending all of our time and all of our money fighting crime when it could be prevented in the classroom."* This was a very prophetic statement in 1791. In 1963 we saw the Bible and prayer taken out of our public schools. From that day we started to see a rise in crime not just in the school, but in society in general. Divorce rates began to rise after several years of decline. Pre-1963 the trouble in schools was chewing gum in class, cutting in line, talking in class and passing notes. Today we have metal detectors because students are bringing guns and knives to school to kill other students and teachers. The NEA claims that there is no correlation, but it all started when prayer and the Bible were removed from our public schools. Our Founding Fathers lived by this scripture: *"For no other foundation can anyone lay than that which is laid, which is*

Bring America Back To Her Religious Roots

Chapter 8 - Their Beliefs

Jesus Christ." - 1 Corinthians 3:11 Without the Great Awakening in the 1730s and the political thinking it generated, we would have had no American Revolution a generation later. Without the Second Great Awakening of the early 19th century and the abolitionist movement that it spawned, we would not have seen the end of slavery a generation later. Similarly, without the courage of many pastors and of groups like the Southern Christian Leadership Conference we would not have seen the civil rights movement of the 1950s and 1960s. Without the pro-life movement Ronald Reagan would not have been elected in 1980, and the Cold War might have gone on. Bill Clinton put a person in charge of "Voice of America". "Voice of America" was a radio broadcast that went into Communist countries and broadcasted world events, Christian programs and other programs that would give people hope for their daily lives and hope for the future. This Clinton appointee stopped all of those programs and instead put on the broadcast Britney Spears

Bring America Back To Her Religious Roots

Chapter 8 - Their Beliefs

and other so-called musicians and even made the statement that the reason the Iron Curtain came down was because of MTV. That is the epitome of stupidity. This person, and so many more in government, have no wisdom because their foundation is not founded on Jesus Christ. Our Founding Fathers proved what could be done when we base ourlives on Jesus and His Word and those people then are placed in government in places of authority. We have gone so far from that belief and to survive as a nation we MUST return. That is our mandate. We have allowed unrighteous men and women to rule over us. Solomon warned about the type of people that rule over us. Proverbs 29:2 *"When the righteous are in authority, the people rejoice: but when the wicked beareth rule, the people mourn."* Bill Clinton vetoed a ban on partial birth abortion twice. He disgraced the office of the presidency in the Oval Office with immoral acts. People may not like the Bible but they love the prosperity, good health, and peace which are the results of

Bring America Back To Her Religious Roots

Chapter 8 - Their Beliefs

obeying its precepts.

Our studies so far have been concerning the extent that our Founding Fathers were influenced by their determination to live according to the moral precepts of not just any religion, but Christianity. We have seen that it was their belief in moral teachings of the Bible that led to the type of government that our nation began with AND it was the rearing of our children on those Biblical teachings that kept our great nation strong and prosperous.

In the last 75 years, with the advent of the ACLU, American's United for the Separation of Church and state, Freedom From Religion Foundation, and others have worked overtime to remove God, the Bible and all vestiges of our religious heritage from public view. All claim that our Constitution declares that we are to do so even though none of our Founding Fathers and the writers of the Constitution were aware of that provision. Most people quote Thomas Jefferson as the one who proves that

Bring America Back To Her Religious Roots
Chapter 8 - Their Beliefs

church and state must be separated even though he never stated that in the context of keeping religion out of government and the public eye. What he did state is this: *"One of the amendments to the Constitution... expressly declares that "Congress shall make no law respecting an establishment of religion, or prohibiting the free exercise thereof, or abridging the freedom of speech, or of the press," thereby guarding in the same sentence and under the same words, the freedom of religion, of speech, and of the press; insomuch that whatever violates either throws down the sanctuary which covers the others."*

We have not been allowed to pray in public schools either as a teacher or as a student for over 40 years. Thomas Jefferson commented about the removal of religious freedoms: *"The rights [to religious freedom] are of the natural rights of mankind, and... if any act shall be... passed to repeal [an act granting those rights] or to narrow its operation, such act will be an infringement of natural right."* Jefferson also commented

Bring America Back To Her Religious Roots

Chapter 8 - Their Beliefs

on government intermeddling in religious affairs: *"I consider the government of the United States as interdicted by the Constitution from intermeddling with religious institutions, their doctrines, discipline, or exercises. This results not only from the provision that no law shall be made respecting the establishment or free exercise of religion, but from that also which reserves to the states the powers not delegated to the United States. Certainly, no power to prescribe any religious exercise or to assume authority in religious discipline has been delegated to the General Government. It must then rest with the states, as far as it can be in any human authority."* We see with this statement that the federal government has no say whatsoever in religious matters. Jefferson also stated: *"No power to prescribe any religious exercise or to assume authority in religious discipline has been delegated to the General Government"*. Yet the courts have declared that a student cannot pray at a graduation ceremony, a teacher cannot have a

Bring America Back To Her Religious Roots

Chapter 8 - Their Beliefs

Bible in his/her desk, or the Ten Commandments cannot be displayed in a classroom. The arrogance of judges today to think that they know more about the meaning of the Constitution than the ones that wrote it is amazing. These activist judges must be removed. The liberties that our Founding Fathers fought and died for are at stake.

Chapter 9

Their Law

Bring America Back To Her Religious Roots

Chapter 9 – Their Law

As we continue in our study of how the Bible influenced the lives of our Founding Fathers AND the establishing of our government, in review, we have seen how the Bible influenced their learning by being **THE** text that all of our Founding Fathers were educated with and we saw how, through their own words, the moral concepts of the Bible directed everything that they did. I now want to look at the place that the Bible is given in the legal profession.

James Wilson, a signer of the Declaration of Independence and a signer of the Constitution (there were only 6 who signed both), was the second most active member at the Constitutional Convention speaking 168 times. After the signing of the Constitution, President Washington placed him as an original justice of the Supreme Court. This was a wise decision to have someone that helped draft the Constitution be a member of the Court that interprets the Constitutional intent. He was the first

Bring America Back To Her Religious Roots
Chapter 9 - Their Laws

one that came up with the idea of formal legal training in America. Up to this time you simply worked with an attorney as an apprentice and after a few years, you took the bar exam. He wrote the first legal texts that were used in the first legal schools in America. In his writings he taught that you not only had to understand civil law, you had to understand the basis of civil law. He states that civil law MUST rest on that law which is divine. He concluded that: *"Far from being rivals, religion and law are twin sisters."* It is the Bible that was the basis for the civil laws of the United States.

1801 is when Fisher Ames, the author of the 1st Amendment which the courts have used to declare separation of church and state, wrote an article about the state of affairs of the public school system: *"It has been the custom of late years to put a number of little books into the hands of children containing fables and moral lessons, This is very well because it is good to raise curiosity and then to guide it, but too much time is being*

Bring America Back To Her Religious Roots

Chapter 9 - Their Laws

spent on these 'frothy' texts and not enough time is being spent on the Bible. The chief textbook in our schools should be the Bible. Why, then, if these new books should be retained, as they will be, why should not the Bible retain the position it once held. Its morals are pure; its examples are captivating and noble. The reverence for the sacred Book that is early impressed lasts long and probably if not impressed in infancy, never take firm hold of the mind." Where can a concept like this be validated in scripture? **Proverbs 22:6** *"Train up a child in the way he should go: and when he is old, he will not depart from it."* Here is the author of the 1st Amendment, the Amendment that our courts of today have used to remove the Bible from the classroom, declaring that the Bible is the best textbook for morals, the best source of instruction and language and general learning.

Elias Boudinot was the president of Congress during the American Revolution and in 1801 he wrote a book titled 'The

Bring America Back To Her Religious Roots

Chapter 9 - Their Laws

Age of Revelation'. *'For nearly half a century I've anxiously and critically studied the Bible and I still scarcely ever take it up that I fail to find something new. Were you to ask me to recommend to you the most valuable book in the world, I should fix on the Bible as the most instructive both to the wise and to the ignorant. Were you to ask me for the book with the most rational and pleasing entertainment to the inquiring mind, I would still say the Bible. And if you should ask again for the best hilosophy or the most interesting history, I would still urge you to look into your Bible. I would make it, in short, the alpha and omega of knowledge."*

This is from one of our most active Founding Fathers. After he served as president of Congress, he went into the 1st Congress and helped frame the Bill of Rights, including the 1st Amendment. This statement from one of the co-authors of the 1st Amendment assures us that the Bible should be allowed in schools as a learning text and not just for its historical facts.

Bring America Back To Her Religious Roots

Chapter 9 - Their Laws

Recently our Supreme Court rejected a case where the Jewish Menorah and the Islamic star and crescent could be displayed during Christmas in New York State public schools, but not the Nativity scene. We have gone a long ways down the wrong road and we must stop and regain the footing that the church once had in this nation. Scripture has warned us about going down this road: Hosea 4:6 *"My people are destroyed for lack of knowledge: because thou hast rejected knowledge, I will also reject thee, that thou shalt be no priest to me: seeing thou hast forgotten the law of thy God, I will also forget thy children."*

In 1808 Benjamin Rush, we've spoke of him earlier concerning the Sunday School movement in 1791, and his belief that all schools should have the Bible as the main teaching text, founded the first American Bible Society who's goal was to put the Bible into the hands of every person in America. This is significant because you will see that within the next eight years 121 Bible societies were started in America. Many of these

Bring America Back To Her Religious Roots
Chapter 9 - Their Laws

societies were started by our Founding Fathers. These are the same Founding Fathers that the revisionist historians try to tell us were atheists and agnostic and deists and did not believe in God and did not believe that religion should be part of everyday life. One of these Founding Fathers was James McHenry, a signer of the Constitution, and Secretary of War. You may recognize that name because of Fort McHenry. That was the fort where Francis Scott Key saw that the flag was still flying after a night of severe naval bombardment and inspired him to write the Star Spangled Banner. McHenry started what is today called the Baltimore Bible society. He believed that the Bible was the best security for the government that he had helped create. *"The Holy Scriptures can alone secure to society order and peace. And to our courts of justice and constitutions of governments purity, stability and usefulness. In vain, without the Bible, we increase our penal laws and draw protections around our institutions."* He believed that unless we lived as a

Bring America Back To Her Religious Roots

Chapter 9 - Their Laws

society, by the Word of God, we could not pass enough laws to protect us from what man will tend to drift towards when left to his own will and emotions. We are seeing that prediction play out today.

What we see today is exactly what he was talking about. When we began to take God out of the schools, out of the workplace, out of government, we began to see more and more laws passed to protect society from itself. In Texas, the Governor has called for all girls from the age of 12 to be vaccinated for a sexually transmitted disease. Parents have no say in the matter; it is required by the state. Why is this? Because we have accepted the behavior of premarital sex even to age of 12 years old!!! We have ignored God's laws and have enacted our own to take its place, but it is too little too late, not to mention totally ineffective.

Our Nation began as a society that lived by the Word of God and to continue to prosper as they did, we have to do what they did, live by the Word of God. If we won't, we will forfeit our rights, our health, our prosperity, our heritage and our nation.

Chapter 10

Their Law (Cont)

Bring America Back To Her Religious Roots

Chapter 10 – Their Law (Cont)

We have begun to look at the influence of the Bible on our legal profession. We saw that scripture was not only the basis of our civil law but our Founding Fathers believed that if man did not know how God governed man, then man could not properly govern man. The Bible was the basis for every aspect of the lives of our Founding Fathers. They maintained the importance of knowing the Bible throughout their lives and saw to it that the Bible was the foundation for the following generations so that each one of those generations would have the same ability to excel, increase, and live in peace.

We have learned that our Founding Fathers, the ones revisionist historians have told us held no belief in God, did not believe in religion and wanted religion to be kept out of the public realm, had started Bible Societies to put into the hands of every American a copy of the Holy Bible.

The most famous Bible Society was the American Bibles

Bring America Back To Her Religious Roots

Chapter 10 - Their Law (Cont.)

Society, which began in 1816 and is still in operation today and distributes 250 million Bibles a year. The first president of American Bibles Society was Elias Boudinot, the 1st President of Congress. One of his vice-presidents was John Jay, the original Chief Justice of the Supreme Court, a General in the Revolutionary War; he was also a president of congress and a diplomat. Matthew Clarkson, a major general during the American Revolution was also one of the vice-presidents as was Smith Thompson, associate justice on the Supreme Court. There are several others who were involved in the founding of this Bible Society that were signers of the Constitution: Presidents, Vice-Presidents, the first Attorney General, Governors, other members of the original Supreme Court, the point is all were Founding Fathers and all were involved in spreading the gospel of Jesus Christ. John Jay, Delegate to the Continental Congress, Member of the New York Constitutional Convention, First Chief Justice of New York, Delegate and

Bring America Back To Her Religious Roots

Chapter 10 - Their Law (Cont.)

elected President of Continental Congress, Minister to Spain, Minister to treat the peace with Great Britain, Secretary of Foreign Affairs, Contributor to The Federalist, First Chief Justice of the Supreme Court of the United States, Negotiator of Jay Treaty with Great Britain, Elected Governor of New York, stated *"The Bible is best of all books, for it is the Word of God. And it teaches us the way to be happy in this world and the next. Continue therefore to read it and to regulate your life by its precepts."* This is the exact opposite of what modern historians are telling us. There is a push to remove the heritage of our religious foundation from the eyes of the public by those who do not like or want religion. They want to bring up generations that have no knowledge of God and His influence on this nation. Their goal is a socialistic society. When you look at the goals of organizations like the ACLU, you see that communism is the ultimate goal. They will deny that but the founder of the ACLU, Roger Baldwin, actually stated that

Bring America Back To Her Religious Roots
Chapter 10 - Their Law (Cont.)

communism was his ultimate goal. The church has not fought to hold the ground that it once had and now we have most of the church, including, the pastors, that have no idea of how much influence the Bible had in the founding of this nation.

Today we can't even say a prayer in the name of Jesus when there is a town meeting, all based on the so-called separation of church and state, but when we review the records or the very early years of this nation we see a much different picture. In 1619 at a meeting of the House of Burgesses it is recorded:

"But, for as much as men's affairs do little prosper when God's service is neglected, all the Burgesses took their places in the Quire till prayer was said by MR. Bucke, the Minister, that it would please God to guide and sanctify all our proceedings to His Own Glory, and the good of this plantation." This document went on to state what was decided at that meeting:

"Be it enacted by this present Assembly that for laying a surer foundation for the conversion of the Indians to Christian

Bring America Back To Her Religious Roots

Chapter 10 - Their Law (Cont.)

religion, each town, city, borough, and particular plantation do obtain unto themselves, by just means, a certain number of natives' children to be educated by them in true religion and a civil course of life. . . " It was even decided in a similar meeting a month later that ALL persons of the settlement were to attend "Divine Services" on the Sabbath or be fined 3 shillings. Can you imagine the lawsuits that type of legislation would bring today? We today do not understand just how important our Founding Fathers and most of the people in their day felt the Bible was to not just their everyday life, but the manner in which the government was designed and run. In the Virginia colony in 1618 they even made the proclamation that obedience was due to the King *as long as* the things he commanded were not against the Word of God. Moving to 1828 we can look at Founding Father Noah Webster. He was a soldier in the American Revolution, a legislator and judge after the Revolution, and one of his main endeavors was to provide

Bring America Back To Her Religious Roots
Chapter 10 - Their Law (Cont.)

learning materials for the younger generations so that they would have the proper education on how this government had been built. For 61 years he spent the majority of his time writing educational books for our public schools. What he is most noted for is the dictionary. That dictionary took him 20 years to write and in the process he also learned 20 different languages. In his definitions of words and to show how they are used he used scripture. About 27% of his definitions used Bible quotes.His 1828 American Dictionary contained the greatest number of Biblical definitions given in any reference volume. Webster considered "education useless without the Bible."

"In my view, the Christian religion is the most important and one of the first things in which all children, under a free government ought to be instructed...No truth is more evident to my mind than that the Christian religion must be the basis of any government intended to secure the rights and privileges of a free people." Webster released his own edition of the Bible in

Bring America Back To Her Religious Roots

Chapter 10 - Their Law (Cont.)

1833, called the Common Version. He used the King James Version as a base and consulted the Hebrew and Greek along with various other versions and commentaries. Webster molded the KJV to correct grammar, replaced words that were no longer used, and did away with words and phrases that could be seen as offensive. Webster was also known to have the entire bible committed to memory.

Chapter 11

Their Bible

Bring America Back To Her Religious Roots

Chapter 11 – Their Bible

Daniel Webster spoke before the Supreme Court in a case in 1844 where a school would not let a minister speak at the school. This brought outrage from the people because the Bible was not allowed in the school as a teaching text. Daniel Webster deliberated in defense of using the Bible before the Supreme Court for three days! Today a lawyer only gets 30 minutes. His case was so decisive that it was printed as a book and distributed all across the Nation. The Courts decision was unanimous 8-0. *"Why should not the Bible and especially the New Testament without note or comment be read or taught as a divine revelation in the school? Its general precepts expounded, its evidences explained, and its glorious principles of morality be inculcated. Where can the purest principles of morality be learned so clearly and so perfectly as from the New Testament?"* The Supreme Court of that day understood that morality could not be taught without the Bible as the source.

Bring America Back To Her Religious Roots

Chapter 11 - Their Bible

They also believed that no government run school should be without the Bible as its main teaching text. Can you imagine a decision like that coming from today's Supreme Court? If it ever decided a case in that manner, the ACLU and all their cronies would be filing lawsuits by the hundreds within the hour.

In 1848, after the death of President John Quincy Adams, a book was published that was a series of letters written by John Quincy Adams to his 10 year old son while he was a diplomat in Russia. He was concerned that his son would not have the proper instruction in studying the Bible while he was in Russia so he sent a series of letters of instruction on how to study the Bible to his son. When these letters became public it was decided that all young people should have this type on instruction. *"The first and only book that deserves universal attention is the Bible. I have made it a practice for many years to read through the Bible once a year. I have always read it*

Bring America Back To Her Religious Roots
Chapter 11 - Their Bible

with the same temper and the same spirit that I extend to you and that is to read it with the intent and desire that it may contribute to my advance in wisdom and virtue." It was John Quincy Adam's intent to learn something that would change his life for the better and it was the Bible that he felt was the best source of wisdom necessary for that. Roger Sherman was the only Founding Father among the 250 to sign all 4 Founding Documents: the Articles of Association, the Articles of Confederation, the Declaration of Independence and the Constitution. He also served in Congress and helped write the Bill of Rights. He also made it a habit to read through the Bible once a year and while he was in Congress he would take a new Bible at the start of each new session and as he would read, he would make notes and at the end of the session he would give the Bible to one of his grand kids.

At the 400th anniversary of Columbus' trip to America in 1892 there was a world's fair type of celebration. At that celebration

Bring America Back To Her Religious Roots
Chapter 11 - Their Bible

there was an exhibit on the growth of education in America and the head of the public schools in Kansas summarized the 400 years of education in this manner: *"The free public schools of America are the outgrowth of the pastoral schools of New England. Nurtured in the lap of the church, these schools soon became so necessary to society at large that the church reluctantly relinquished her claim on these schools. Whether this was wise or not is not my purpose to discuss, if the study of the Bible is to be excluded from all state schools, if the inculcation of the principles of Christianity is to have no place in the daily program, and the worship of God is to have no part of the general exercise of these public schools, then the good of the state would be better served to restore all schools to church control."*

In the textbook "History of the United States" written by Noah Webster and used in our schools for 150 years he states, *"All the miseries and evils which men suffer from vice, crime,*

Bring America Back To Her Religious Roots

Chapter 11 - Their Bible

ambition, injustice, oppression, slavery, and war they are perceived from despising or neglecting the precepts contained in the Bible."

John Adams – *"Suppose that a distant nation should take the Bible as its only law book. And suppose that they would regulate his conduct by the precepts in the Bible. What a utopia, what a paradise this region would be."*

John Jay – *"The Bible is the best of all books. It is the Word of God. Continue therefore to read it and to regulate your life by its precepts."*

This is how our Founding Fathers built this nation. This is how they laid the foundation for the greatest nation this world has ever or will ever see. It is laid on the Gospel of Jesus Christ and unless we get back to where we need to be in depending on God's Word for everything like they did, we will lose everything they gave their all for.

As we have seen over the last few chapters, the sentiment

Bring America Back To Her Religious Roots
Chapter 11 - Their Bible

towards Christianity has taken a turn for the worse. There are those who have deemed it their life's purpose to destroy the religious foundation that our nation was built on. It isn't surprising that some of these people are supposed ministers either. Today too many ministers are completely ignorant of the role that Christianity played in establishing this country. This year will be the 400th anniversary of the founding of Jamestown, VI. But this year's celebration will be a little different. There doesn't seem to be the love of country that there once was. For nearly 200 years, our leaders have recognized the importance of celebrating the providential goodness of the Lord Jesus Christ through our nation's birth in Jamestown in 1607. But this year's Quadricentennial, officials are intent on belittling our nation's Christian heritage and referring to the Jamestown settlers as bloodthirsty cannibals, environmental terrorists, and even worse. They have gone so far as to ban the word 'celebration' because, after all, as one

Bring America Back To Her Religious Roots

Chapter 11 - Their Bible

official stated, *"You can't celebrate an invasion."*

At the State of the Black Union Jamestown Conference, Rev. Otis Moss, as part of a panel discussion with Rev.'s Al Sharpton and Jesse Jackson, invoked a highly charged comparison to Nazism and the KKK, declaring that the Jamestown settlers were guilty of mass 'holocaust' and 'lynchings'. This is how they described Captain John Smith, Pocahantas and the rest of the Virginia Company, which is totally unfounded, inaccurate and irresponsible. This is the type of teaching that goes on today. There is no reference to the actual history of our nation, just what some revisionist historians want it to be.

Chapter 12

Their Stand

Bring America Back To Her Religious Roots

Chapter 12 – Their Stand

William and Mary was the 2nd college in the American colonies. It was chartered in 1693 and Rev. James Blair was its first president. Needless to say, it was founded as a Christian college. Just this last year, the president of William and Mary removed the cross that adorned the Wren Chapel, because he felt that it could offend those who were not of the Christian faith. After 314 years as a Christian college, they are now afraid that the cross may offend somebody. The president, Gene Nichol (President, North Florida ACLU, 1984; Chair, University of Colorado Task Force on Gay and Lesbian Issues, 1992-93; Colorado Democrat of the Year, 1999; Member, Board of Directors, North Carolina Civil Liberties Union (2002); Colorado ACLU (1999- 2000); Keynote Address Speaker, North Carolina - American Civil Liberties Union annual banquet, North Carolina, October, 2004.), needs to read Romans 1:16 *"For I am not ashamed of the gospel of Jesus*

Bring America Back To Her Religious Roots

Chapter 12 - Their Stand

Christ, for it is the power of God unto salvation to everyone who believes. . . " This decision cost the college dearly. Many stopped their donations to the college; one was for $12 million. This got the attention of Mr. Nichol and he will now display the cross, but only in a limited manner. Why is there such a fear of anything Christian? As I've stated before, there is no fear of Islam, no push to keep it out of schools. New York State will have the nation's only Islamic public school, teaching Islam with most of the classes being taught in Arabic and paid for by the taxpayers of New York and nobody, not even the ACLU has a problem with that. Why? Because Islam is not a threat to the true church's enemy, Satan. Islam is Satan's cohort. Hinduism is Satan's cohort, Buddhism is Satan's cohort, but Christianity is Satan's enemy. Christianity is the ONLY religion that can defeat Satan. Christianity is the only religion that can do any damage to Satan's kingdom; therefore Christianity is the only religion that is attacked by the unreligious. This is why so

Bring America Back To Her Religious Roots
Chapter 12 - Their Stand

many people are trying to rewrite history attempting to show that Christianity had nothing to do with how this nation was born.

When you take the time to study our history, *something that the revisionists don't want you to do*, you will find that every aspect of the lives of the people involved the Bible. Every major college was started by churches. William and Mary, Harvard, Yale, Dartmouth, Princeton, which celebrates the fact that many of the signers of the Constitution graduated from Princeton, James Madison, Richard Stockton, Benjamin Rush, Gunning Bedford, Jonathan Dayton and many more. Princeton was originally a seminary. King's College, now called Columbia University, founded in 1754, and was very strong in the belief that Christianity was the most important part of a person's life. The commencement speech given to the graduates by its first president, Founder and signer of the Constitution, William Samuel Johnson affirms this belief: *"You this day, gentlemen,*

Bring America Back To Her Religious Roots
Chapter 12 - Their Stand

have received a public education, the purpose whereof hath been to qualify you the better to serve your Creator and your country. . . Your first great duties, you are sensible, are those you owe to heaven, to your Creator, and Redeemer. Let these be ever present to your minds and exemplified in your lives and conduct. Imprint deep upon your minds the principles of piety towards God and a reverence and fear of His Holy Name. The fear of God is the beginning of wisdom. Remember, too, that you are redeemed of the Lord, that you are bought with a price, even the inestimable price of the precious blood of the Son of God. . . Love, fear, and serve Him as your Creator, Redeemer, and Sanctifier. Acquaint yourselves with Him in His Word and holy ordinances. Make Him your friend and protector and your felicity is secured both here and the hereafter."

Rutgers University was founded by a pastor. By 1860 there were 246 colleges founded and all but 17 were founded by different religious denominations. These religious

Bring America Back To Her Religious Roots

Chapter 12 - Their Stand

denominations were all Christian denominations.

George Washington, which many of the modern day revisionists claim was a deist, commented to Chiefs of the Delaware Indian tribes when they brought three Indian youths to be trained in American schools; *"You do well to wish to learn our arts and ways of life, and above all, the religion of Jesus Christ. These will make you a greater and happier people than you are. Congress will do everything they can to assist you in this wise intention."* Here, Congress is involved in teaching the Christian religion to American Natives. The total fallacy of the teaching that our young nation was not a Christian nation is an inexcusable and outright lie. Samuel Adams and Richard Henry Lee of Virginia formed the Committees of Correspondence to educate the populace as to what the status was concerning the struggle with Britain and to give inspiration to those loyal to America. Samuel Adams wrote a piece called "The Rights of the Colonists" and in that work he stated: *"The Rights of the*

Bring America Back To Her Religious Roots

Chapter 12 - Their Stand

Colonists as Christians may best be understood by reading and carefully studying the institutes of the Great Law Giver and Head of the Christian Church, which are to be found clearly written ad promulgated in the New Testament."

The spiritual nature of the American resistance to the oppression of England was so clear that during debates in the British Parliament it was brought forth by Sir Richard Sutton . . . *"If you ask an American, "Who is his master?" He will tell you he has none, nor any governor, but Jesus Christ."* That is not a statement from an atheist, or a deist, but from a believer in Jesus Christ. At the time of the Boston Tea Party when Parliament passed the Boston Port Bill to blockade Boston harbor, to eliminate all trade to and from one of America's key ports, the news reports in Great Britain reported: *"The province of Virginia appointed the 1st day of June, the day on which the Boston Port Bill took place, to be set aside for fasting and prayer and humiliation, to implore the Divine interposition to*

Bring America Back To Her Religious Roots

Chapter 12 - Their Stand

avert the heavy calamity which threatened destruction to their civil rights with the evils of civil war, and to give one heart and one mind to the people firmly to oppose every injury to the American rights. This example was either followed or a similar resolution adopted almost everywhere and the 1st of June became a day of prayer and humiliation throughout the continent." This is an action of believers. This is the mindset of the members of the Body of Christ. This is the direction that the church today needs to go. We have to rise up and stand for our rights, the rights that our forefathers fought and died for. Little by little we have had our religious freedoms taken away from us. It has been so subtle that some have not even noticed. The greatest threat we face is the complacency of the Body of Christ.At the start of the American Revolution Congress passed the Articles of War to govern the Continental Army. In it were these directives: *It is earnestly recommended to all officers and soldiers diligently to attend Divine service; and all officers and*

Bring America Back To Her Religious Roots

Chapter 12 - Their Stand

soldiers who shall behave indecently or irreverently at any place of Divine worship, shall . . . be brought before a court-martial. Now days, we court-martial a Christian chaplain who prays in the Name of Jesus. We have come a long way in the wrong direction and have a long way to go to get back to where the church is supposed to be.

Chapter 13

The Signs of Apostasy

Bring America Back To Her Religious Roots

Chapter 13 – The Signs of Apostasy

If the church does not influence the people in the proper way, the nation will drift down the wrong path as we have seen the U. S. do since 1954. If we allow the ungodly to influence society, we will allow ungodly men and women to control our lives and the influence on our lives, as we have seen, will be perversion, intolerance and outright hatred for Christianity.

The time has come for all men to make a stand against all the ungodly things of this world and stand up for what built our nation, the Gospel of Jesus Christ!

As we have been studying the religious history of the US and the influence of the Bible on the Founding Fathers and literally most of the people of their day, we have seen that they were not afraid to incorporate the Christian values into the government and its policies and its civil laws. We have also seen that the Bible was THE book of influence in ALL schools; public, private and even most of the colleges and universities were

Bring America Back To Her Religious Roots

Chapter 13 - The Signs of Apostasy

started by Christian denominations for the development of and propagation of the Gospel of Jesus Christ. We have drifted a long ways from those roots. Today a liberal college professor has to be threatened with a lawsuit just to grade a paper from a student with a Christian prospective. A Southern Illinois University professor refused to grade or pass a student in her class because the student did not agree with the professor's viewpoint on abortion. This is the way the liberal left addresses the issues. Outlaw your opposition so they **have** to think the way you think. After a lawsuit was filed by a Christian organization on behalf of the student, the so-called professor issued a passing grade so the student could graduate. But they call the Christian religion intolerant, yet they refuse to allow thinking that is contrary to what they want you to think. When we look at the state that our society is in, we have to ask why we have gone so far to the left and so far away from God and His way of doing things. I believe that the answer to that is

Bring America Back To Her Religious Roots

Chapter 13 - The Signs of Apostasy

simple; the church has not stood its ground when it comes to upholding moral character.

Yes, even the church has had its problems with some of our Christian leaders going stray because of the lust of the eye and ending up inscandalous affairs. It's when we don't recognize immoral behavior as sin and repent of sin that we begin to go down a path that leads to destruction.

We have such a division within our society concerning what is right and what is wrong. This division has gone all the way into the church and into politics. Some churches see no problem with homosexuality and even ordain practicing homosexuals to preach. Then there is the true church that actually believes the Word of God and teaches that homosexuality is a sin. In the political arena we have one party that requires a member to resign if they have been involved in something that may have been either questionable or illegal. If it turns out that the person did something illegal, the supporters of that party usually do not vote the person back into office. The other party, however, has a totally different set of rules. They demand the resignation of the opposing party's offender, but not if one of their own is involved in an illegal act. We saw this last year when a member of the house was filmed accepting a bribe. The bills were marked and recorded and later $90,000.00 of that bribe money was found in his freezer. He was not asked by his party to step aside. He was even voted back into office. There doesn't seem to be a sense of right and wrong. This official was defeated in a subsequent election and then convicted of bribery. One party demands that all of their members hold fast to what is right, and the other party demands that they don't have to be held accountable for anything.

If you ask, "Who is responsible?" the only answer is the church. We have failed to hold fast to the commandment of God. We have allowed the worlds views on things to slip into the church. It has been said that however the church goes, the nation goes.

Bring America Back To Her Religious Roots

Chapter 13 - The Signs of Apostasy

With so many in the so-called religious arena that totally disregard the Word of God and preach whatever they want, it is no wonder that there is so much confusion.

When our forefathers came to this land they held fast to what the Word of God said. They didn't question it, they just lived by it. They didn't allow people to live together without the benefit of marriage. Teen age girls were not getting pregnant at 11 and 12.

Homosexuals were not allowed to be ordained. They didn't teach their young children that homosexuality was a viable lifestyle in the public schools; they didn't hand out condoms to 10 year olds. All of this has happened because the church has given up control of the raising of our children to people who don't have enough sense to come in out of the rain. We have given up control of society so that people do whatever they feel like doing. When I was growing up we used to say, "If it feels good, do it!" Well, we did and now look at the society we

Bring America Back To Her Religious Roots
Chapter 13 - The Signs of Apostasy

created. Soft porn on the TV all the time, 11 and 12 year old girls getting pregnant, in this last election we almost made possession of pot legal, God has been kicked out of the schools and now we have metal detectors in the schools. It just keeps getting worse and the church, as a whole, just sits back and complains but does nothing. When will the church realize that it is their responsibility to take back control? God will judge those who have led the people astray, but He will hold the church responsible for allowing that to happen. Jeremiah 23:1 warns pastors: *"Woe be unto the pastors that destroy and scatter the sheep of my pasture! saith the LORD."* Too many feel that because we are in the last days that there is nothing that can be done. That is not true. Just because we are in the last days does not mean that we just sit back and do nothing. You can't be the light of the world when you aren't doing anything. Don't let our legislators pass legislation that is against the Word of God. Don't sit back and let the homosexual community force

Bring America Back To Her Religious Roots

Chapter 13 - The Signs of Apostasy

their perverted lifestyle on all of society. Force Washington to allow the Bible back into the schools. Force our places of higher education to replace the liberal, socialist thinking professor with God fearing conservative, constitutionally minded professors. Recall the judges that want to allow the vilest of sex education in our schools, that use international law instead of our Constitution to define our laws and deprive parents the right to raise their kids in a God fearing environment. Recall judges that tell parents they have no say in what the public schools teach their children and that have taken away the right of the parent to know about medical procedures their children are having.

Chapter 14

The Pastors

Bring America Back To Her Religious Roots

Chapter 14 – The Pastors

To think that today's government would allow the Christian religion to strongly influence its decisions is not hard to do. The removal of 100 of the ungodly men and women that have influence in Washington is all it would take. It's not like our government was never influenced by Christianity in the past. On September 11, 1777 it was requested of Congress to print or import Bibles: *"That the use of the Bible is so universal, and its importance so great . . . your Committee recommend that Congress will order the Committee of Commerce to import 20,000 Bibles from Holland, Scotland, or elsewhere, into different ports of the States of the Union."* Congress agreed and ordered the Bibles.

On March 28, 1778 the General Assembly of Vermont asked the Rev. Peter Powers to address them in an 'election sermon' (a discourse on the application of Biblical principles to civil government). His message "Jesus Christ, the True King and

Bring America Back To Her Religious Roots

Chapter 14 – The Pastors

Head of Government" based on Matt. 28:18 was so stirring that The General Assembly of Vermont ordered it printed and distributed it among the people of Vermont. The church and pastors in particular were of the utmost importance during the Revolutionary war. Today's so-called historians want us to think that Christianity had no influence at all on the people or the government, but that could not be farther from the truth. The pastors were effective from both sides of the pulpit. From the backside they would build the people up and provide Biblical guidance with topical sermons, election sermons and even artillery sermons, a discourse on the application of Biblical principles to the military. For those who believe that Christians are not supposed to go to war have never read the Bible. Ecclesiastes tells us that there is a time of peace and a time of war. Jesus said to the ones He sent out to preach, if you don't have a sword, sell your tunic and buy one. We aren't supposed to let people walk all over us. John Adams stated that there

Bring America Back To Her Religious Roots

Chapter 14 – The Pastors

were two ministers in particular that were extremely ardent and influential in awakening a revival of American principles and feelings, Rev. Dr. Mayhew and the Rev. Dr. Cooper. From the front side of the pulpit you usually found the pastor directing the troops as military leaders and officers. Rev. John Peter Muhlenberg of Virginia preached a message on January 21, 1776 concerning the crisis that was facing America. He reminded them of how America was founded in the pursuit of religious and civil liberties and how they were now in danger of losing those hard fought for liberties. He concluded with these words:

"In the language of the Holy Writ there is a time for all things, a time to preach and a time to pray, but those times have passed away. There is a time to fight- and that time has come!"

His sermon finished, he offered the benediction and then proceeded to disrobe in front of the congregation, revealing a

Bring America Back To Her Religious Roots

Chapter 14 – The Pastors

military uniform of a military officer beneath his robes. He called for recruits and 300 men joined him becoming the 8th Virginia Regiment.

There were so many clergy in the war that the British called them the "Black Regiment", because of the usual black robes they wore as preachers. George Washington addressed his troops as the winter at Valley Forge was leaving: *"While we are zealously performing the duties of good citizens and soldiers, we certainly ought not to be inattentive to the higher duties of religion. To the distinguished character of Patriot, it should be our highest glory to add the more distinguished character of Christian."*

We have let our heritage be pushed back into a closet. We can bring it back to the forefront. We MUST bring it back to the forefront. We can remove the ungodly politicians that we have put into office and replace them with Godly, righteous, spirit filled men and women of God that are not afraid to legislate according to the commandments of God. I'm not calling for a theocracy, just a government based on Biblical principles, the same that our Founding Fathers envisioned and established.

2 Chronicles 7:14 *"If my people, which are called by my name, shall humble themselves, and pray, and seek my face, and turn from their wicked ways; then will I hear from heaven, and will forgive their sin, and will heal their land."* We have seen in this study a completely different America than what the new revisionist historians have tried to make us believe. We have seen that the Bible was the most important book for their personal lives, business lives, civil law, foundation for our government, and even for military government. It was very important to our Founding Fathers to make sure that our military personnel reflected the Christian lifestyle in their actions. Samuel Adams made this comment in 1780: *"May every citizen in the army and in the country have a proper sense of Deity upon his mind and an impression of the declaration*

Bring America Back To Her Religious Roots

Chapter 14 – The Pastors

recorded in the Bible, "Him that honoreth me I will honor, but he that despiseth me shall be lightly esteemed." 1 Samuel 2.30"

In October of 1781 the Americans won the Battle of Yorktown in which the British laid down their arms. This was the decisive battle of the Revolutionary War. The British press reported the event as follows: *"It was on the 19th of October that Lord Cornwallis surrendered himself and his whole army. . . . Two days after the capitulation took place, Divine service was performed in all the different brigades and divisions of the American army in order to return thanks to the Almighty for this great event; and it was recommended by General Washington to all the troops that were not upon duty, in his general orders, that they would assist at "Divine service" with serious deportment and with that sensibility of heart which the recollection of the surprising and particular interposition of Providence in their favor claimed."* General Washington wanted all to pay tribute to Almighty God for the great favor for

Bring America Back To Her Religious Roots

Chapter 14 – The Pastors

which He had bestowed upon America. They had just defeated the mightiest army in the world and they had done it with a ragtag army of volunteers.

Congress even got involved on October 24, 1781 and set aside a time to honor God. *"Resolved, That Congress will at two o'clock this day go in procession to the Dutch Lutheran Church and return thanks to Almighty God for crowning the allied armies of the United States and France with success by the surrender of the whole British Army under the command of Earl Cornwallis."* Oh, for a Congress with the courage of these men.

Chapter 15

How It Works

Bring America Back To Her Religious Roots

Chapter 15 – How It Works

The treaty between America and England, which took two years to finalize, acknowledged the strong Christian heritage of our Founding Fathers. It began "In the Name of the most holy and undivided Trinity. . ."

Today it seems that any proclamation by the government that references religion brings a ton of lawsuits claiming the separation of church and state clause that isn't in our Constitution. When word reached America concerning the finalization of the treaty, there was a celebration planned. Congress assigned three people to prepare a proclamation for a day of prayer and thanksgiving. Congress approved the proclamation and distributed it among the states. This proclamation stated:

"Whereas is has pleased the Supreme Ruler of all human events to dispose the hearts of the belligerent powers to put a period to the infusion of human blood proclaiming a cessation of all

Bring America Back To Her Religious Roots

Chapter 15 – How It Works

hostilities by sea and land . . . And whereas in the progress of a contest on which the most essential rights of human nature depended, the interposition of Divine Providence in our favor has been most abundantly and most graciously manifested, and the citizens of these United States have every reason for praise and gratitude to the God of their salvation. Impressed, therefore, with an exalted sense in the blessings by which we are surrounded, and of our entire dependence on that Almighty Being from whose goodness and bounty they are derived, the United States in Congress assembled, do recommend to the several states. . . a day of public thanksgiving that all the people may then assemble to celebrate with grateful hearts and united voices the praises of their Supreme and all bountiful Benefactor for His numberless favors and mercies . . . and above all that He has been pleased to continue to us the light of the blessed Gospel and secure to us in the fullest extent the rights of conscience in faith and worship."

Bring America Back To Her Religious Roots

Chapter 15 – How It Works

Today's Congress would not issue a statement of this nature for two reasons. First, they do not want the lawsuits that would flood the courts from the ACLU and its allies and second, there are not that many in Congress that would actually have the convictions to make a statement of that nature. During the designing of the Constitution in Philadelphia, they spent long hours and many weeks preparing the correct wording of our Constitution. When, after many days of no progress, our non-religious forefathers, as today's so-called historians like to call them, recorded a very stirring speech made by the 81 year old Benjamin Franklin where he called for the Convention to call upon Providence. *"I have lived a long time, sir, and the longer I live, the more convincing proofs I see of this truth – that God governs the affairs of men. And if a sparrow cannot fall to the ground without His notice, is it probable that an empire can rise without His aid? We have been assured, sir, in the Sacred Writings, that "Except the Lord build the house, they labor in*

Bring America Back To Her Religious Roots
Chapter 15 – How It Works

vain to build it." Then he declared the need to call a minister in for counsel. This speech is striking because it was made by one of the least religious of the Founding Fathers. This motion was tabled ONLY because the Convention did not have the funds to pay the minister, however several personal accounts of the remainder of the Convention did note that prayer was made before each session began. It is obvious by these examples that our Founding Fathers neither precluded nor limited public expression or official religious acknowledgments. We have seen through the writings of the Founding Fathers, the actions of the Founding Fathers and the beliefs of the Founding Fathers that their religion, Christianity, was the guiding force in their lives. They allowed the Word of God to be THE dominate guide of their affairs. Today we see organizations like the ACLU doing everything that they can to separate any form of religion from government AND public domain. Was this what our Founding Fathers wanted? Is this how they ran their

Bring America Back To Her Religious Roots

Chapter 15 – How It Works

affairs? I want to look at the first inauguration that occurred in 1789. The New York Daily Advertiser reported the event as follows: *"On the morning of the day in which our illustrious President will be invested with his office, the bells will ring at 9 o'clock, when the people may go up to the house of God and in a solemn manner commit the new government, with its important train of consequences, to the holy protection and blessing of the Most High. An early hour is prudently fixed for this peculiar act of devotion and is designed wholly for prayer."* After the oath of office was given the Senate and the members of the House of Representatives, the President and vice-President all went to St. Paul's Chapel to hear Divine Service. **This was done by Resolution by the Senate**. It was done by a unanimous vote. I would propose the question that if there was to be a total separation of church and state, then why would Congress resolve to have the entire United States government at the time attend a church service? Another interesting question

Bring America Back To Her Religious Roots

Chapter 15 – How It Works

concerning the separation of church and state is on the same day that Congress approved the 1st Amendment, they requested that President Washington designate a national day of thanksgiving. This day was to be spent giving thanks to Almighty God, not Mohammed or Buddha, but THE God of the universe, the maker of heaven and earth. President Washington concurred and on October 3, 1789 he declared a day of thanksgiving. After the Revolution and the forming of our government, it was a wonder to many foreigners the rapid rise as a successful nation that the United States enjoyed. They were still in amazement as to how a small nation of farmers and merchants were able to defeat what was arguably the world's greatest military power. They were also amazed at how we could form a government so quickly that was envied across the globe.

To answer these questions, many writers came to America and traveled about studying our government and just how the American people lived their lives. They would then report what

Bring America Back To Her Religious Roots

Chapter 15 – How It Works

they had discovered to their countrymen. One such visitor was Edward Kendall. He traveled across America from 1807 to 1808 and then returned to England where in 1809 he published his notes on his travels entitled, *Travels in America*. Here is how he described "election day" in Connecticut in 1807: *"At about eleven o'clock, his Excellency Governor Jonathan Trumball entered the statehouse and shortly after took his place at the head of a procession which was made to a meetinghouse or church at something less than a half a mile distance. The procession was made on foot and was composed of a person of the governor, together with the lieutenant-governor, assistants, high sheriffs, members of the lower house of assembly, and, unless with accidental exceptions, all the clergy of the state. The pulpit or, as it is called here, the desk, was filled by three if not four clergymen; a number which, by its form and dimensions, it was able to accommodate. Of these, one opened the service with prayer; another delivered the sermon; a third*

Bring America Back To Her Religious Roots
Chapter 15 – How It Works

made a concluding prayer; and a fourth pronounced a benediction. Several hymns were sung; and, among others, an occasional one [a special one for that occasion]. The total number of singers was between forty and fifty. The sermon, as will be supposed, touched upon matters of government. When all was finished, the procession returned to the statehouse."

The point in this dissertation I want you to see is that all of the state government attended the religious service. Yes, it was an election period, but the religious foundation they had was very prevalent in the ceremony that Kendall witnessed. It is what we need to see again.

Chapter 16

The Practice

Bring America Back To Her Religious Roots

Chapter 16 – The Practice

In the last chapter I began to show you what outsiders saw within America shortly after the Revolutionary War. I included that entire description for the purpose of pointing out that all of the members of the government attended the church service and the minister preached a message on Biblical government. This, according to revisionist historians, would not have occurred because our Founding Fathers, in their opinion, were not Christians. But it is a history that DID happen. The accounts of these types of functions are not just an isolated event but something that happened throughout young America. It was a history that involved the Christian pastors of every city and township in America. The vital link between Christianity and our government is something that cannot be ignored. John Quincy Adams stated: *"The highest glory of the American Revolution was this: it connected in one indissoluble bond the principles of civil government with the principles of*

Bring America Back To Her Religious Roots

Chapter 16 – The Practice

Christianity." This is the history that we, the pastors, must reintroduce to America. As further proof of this "indissoluble bond" let's take a look at another 'outsider' whose visit to America twenty five years later confirmed what Kendall discovered in 1808. Frenchman Alex de Tocqueville visited America in the 1830's and studied the American life and government and in 1835 published what is now called *Democracy in America*. His findings would make the ACLU's founder turn over in his grave. He observed: *"Upon my arrival to the United States, the religious aspect of the country was the first thing that struck my attention; and the longer I stayed there, the more did I perceive the great political consequences resulting from this state of things, to which I was unaccustomed. In France I had almost always seen the spirit of religion and the spirit of freedom pursuing courses diametrically opposed to each other;* ***but in America I found that they are intimately united, and that they reigned in common over the same***

Bring America Back To Her Religious Roots
Chapter 16 – The Practice

country." (Emphases mine)

Our revisionist historians have revised Alex de Tocqueville's *Democracy in America* in a reprint done by Richard D. Heffner in an edition explained as "Specially Edited and Abridged for the Modern Reader." It contains less than half of the original text and what was left out was most of de Tocqueville's comments on the family, morality, and religion. The comment listed above was eliminated.

This comment was eliminated: *"The Americans combine the notions of Christianity and of liberty so intimately in their minds that it is impossible to make them conceive the one without the other."*

Our history books no longer teach the real history of our Founders nor of their faith. This is how revisionists remove religion from the minds of the people. They simply do not talk about it. They give very little if any reference to it. One school book has 30 pages on the Pilgrims that includes the first

Bring America Back To Her Religious Roots
Chapter 16 – The Practice

Thanksgiving. But there is no reference at all as to Christianity being part of the Pilgrims life. One high-school level text listed 83 important dates in America and only one was religious. Early educators believe that to omit religious elements and a Providential view of history would do nothing but deprive students of the true history of America. Charles Coffin, an author of student history texts in the 1870's, stated: *"There is still one other point [to the teaching of history]: you will notice that while the oppressors have carried out their plans and had things their own way, there were forces silently at work which in time undermined their plans, as if a Divine hand were directing the counter plan. Whoever pursues the "Story of Liberty" without recognizing this feature will fail of fully comprehending the meaning of history. There must be a meaning to history or else existence is an incomprehensible enigma (complete riddle)."*

The reason for the elimination of religion from history is to

Bring America Back To Her Religious Roots

Chapter 16 – The Practice

indoctrinate generations to expect and then demand a society that is devoid of public displays of religion in any form. Monuments such as the Ten Commandments, crosses on mountain sides, prayer at city council meetings or school graduations must be outlawed for this to be effective. This type of maneuvering over the last 75 years by the ACLU and others have many people believing that our First Amendment actually calls for no public display of religion or religious monuments. We have seen that prayer was a major part of the lives of our Founding Fathers. All of Congress attended divine services before attending to business or at least having a prayer made in the Name of Jesus before the start of each session. There was no "separation of church and state" practiced by our Founding Fathers. In fact, the exact opposite is true. They intertwined their faith with the government to insure that God was part of the daily affairs in both private life and the affairs of government. They wanted and needed His guidance and were

Bring America Back To Her Religious Roots

Chapter 16 – The Practice

not afraid to act accordingly. Too bad our Congress today is too proud and arrogant to seek His help.

All through this study we have looked at how the religious faith of our Founding Fathers influenced not just their daily lives but also the civil laws of this nation, the manner in which a politician would govern himself as a leader of the people and it was also the foundation for the framing of the Constitution of the United States.

We do not have the time to study the lives of each of the 250 Founding Fathers, but we should look at a few of the statements that today's revisionists have attributed to our Founding Fathers. One of these statements is from John Adams – *"This would be the best of all possible worlds if there were no religion at all."* What the revisionists do [NOT] tell you is what he said next; *"But in this exclamation I would have been as fanatical as Bryant and Cleverly. Without religion this world would be something not fit to be mentioned in polite company, I mean*

Bring America Back To Her Religious Roots

Chapter 16 – The Practice

hell." A statement taken completely out of context and made a veritable lie to make it appear that one of our Founding Fathers was not the Christian that he really was. Another quote that is often used is one attributed to George Washington. *"The government of the United States is in no sense founded on the Christian religion."* This phrase was taken from a treaty with Tripoli, a Muslim nation, in 1797. The biggest problem with this statement is George Washington didn't say it or write it. This treaty was not the work of Washington as he had nothing to do with it. The other problem with that statement is it is taken out of context and references the ***federal government*** which supports no religion making the statement true. But without the rest of the treaty it was taken from it leads the reader to believe that America had no religious basis which is why they use that statement. This treaty was ratified under the Presidential term of John Adams. It would be absurd to suggest that President Adams would have endorsed any provision that

Bring America Back To Her Religious Roots

Chapter 16 – The Practice

repudiated Christianity. To prove this, while discussing the conflict that brought about the treaty with Thomas Jefferson, Adams declared: *"The policy of Christendom has made cowards of all the sailors before the standard of Mahomet. It would be heroical and glorious in us to restore courage to ours."*

It was also Adams that stated: *"The general principles on which the fathers achieved independence were . . . the general principles of Christianity . . . I will avow that I believe then, and now believe, that those general principles of Christianity are as eternal and immutable as the existence and attributes of God; and that those principles of liberty are as unalterable as human nature."*

Our history has been rewritten by those that want to make America a secular nation and we have allowed it. We need to demand that the real history be taught and that includes our

Bring America Back To Her Religious Roots
Chapter 16 – The Practice

religious heritage. I will say this again because we must never forget, if we don't remember who we were; we will not know who we are.

Chapter 17

The Fight

Bring America Back To Her Religious Roots

Chapter 17 – The Fight

Thomas Paine wrote a book called *Age of Reason* in which he attacked religion in general and Christianity in particular. This book was met with scathing rebuke from Ben Franklin, John Jay (1st Chief Justice), John Adams, Samuel Adams, Ben Rush and John Dickinson (signers of the Declaration of Independence), Patrick Henry, Zephaniah Swift (author of America's 1st law book). Many others rebuked Paine for his book, but even he stated in that book that he believed in one God.

Ben Franklin summarized the character of America to the French in this manner: *"Bad examples of youth are more rare in America, which must be comfortable consideration to parents. To this may be truly added, that serious religion, under its various denominations, is not only tolerated, but respected and practiced. Atheism is unknown there, infidelity (a disbelief in Scriptures and in Christianity) rare and secret; so that persons may live to a great age in that country, without having their*

Bring America Back To Her Religious Roots

Chapter 17 – The Fight

piety shocked by meeting with either an atheist or infidel." In this installment of this series, I would like to point to the importance of following the example that our Founding Fathers set forth for us to follow. They purposely lived so that their lives would be an example for unborn generations to follow. They set down a manner in which, if followed, would produce the same results all the time. Throughout this study we have found that the revisionists of today have taught us and our children nothing but lies concerning the depth of the importance that Christianity played in the everyday lives of the Founding Fathers. There are reasons for their telling these lies. There are those today that are trying to turn America into a socialistic nation. They have, for 70 years, used our laws against us, rewrote history with blatant lies, and have even attempted to make illegal the telling of the true history of the United States. They have successfully removed most of the religious heritage from the public domain. Without being reminded of that

Bring America Back To Her Religious Roots

Chapter 17 – The Fight

heritage, there are those who never learn the truth about our history. I blame the church for its failure to stop the liberal slide that began in the 1920's with the founding of the ACLU. They did not seem to fear the subtleness of this enemy of the church and civilization as a whole or they just didn't see it. They have not discerned that our spiritual enemy has been able to infiltrate the church and take it off in a direction that will surely result in many souls lost for eternity.

As the church goes, so goes the nation. If the church is able to be led in the wrong direction, then the nation will follow. If we elect leaders that are good for the economy, but have no regard for the things of God in the social issues, our nation will collapse. They won't be any good for the nation or the economy. Our leaders will determine the direction of the nation. An example of this is when Bill Clinton was President. He was involved in several lawsuits because of his womanizing. The details of his tryst with Monica Lewinski became public

Bring America Back To Her Religious Roots

Chapter 17 – The Fight

and he tried to deny it. His attempt to deny that what he did was of a sexual nature created a drastic rise in that particular behavior among our young children and because *he* said it wasn't sex they thought that it was OK. We have had several presidents that have disgraced that office with infidelity and all seem to be of the same party. It is that same party that has allowed and continues to support the murdering of our unborn. It is that same party that is trying to force the acceptance of homosexual marriage of the people of the United States. It is that same party that has tried for years and is attempting at this moment to make the reading of scripture that condemns homosexuality a hate crime that will put any preacher that stands on the biblical teaching of homosexuality in jail. It is that same party that is trying, as we speak, to disallow our Constitutional right of correcting the direction of the government by keeping the general population apprised of what is going on in Washington. It is that same party that has ignored

Bring America Back To Her Religious Roots

Chapter 17 – The Fight

the directives of the former President concerning foreign policy and has usurped the authority of our President simply because they don't like his policy. In all of this the church, for the most part remains silent.

During WWII in Germany, the church didn't say much about book burning because it wasn't the Bible that was being burned. The church didn't say much when the minorities and mentally ill were being sent off to concentration camps. The church didn't say much when cults were outlawed and the members of the cults were shipped off to concentration camps. The church didn't even say much when the Jews were rounded up and sent to the gas chambers. Then Germany came after the church and there was no one left to defend her. We are seeing the same thing happen today in the US. Little by little our rights are being taken away. Two years ago in Connecticut the right to own property without the fear of the government taking it away from you was overruled. Any government that wants your

Bring America Back To Her Religious Roots
Chapter 17 – The Fight

property so a developer can build something that creates more taxes for the city now has the right to take your property and give it to a developer. The 5th Amendment has become null and void. The biggest reason for this Supreme Court ruling was to be able to take property away from churches. Churches don't create tax revenues so they want to be able to take property from anyone if they can generate more revenue with it. All through this the church stays, for the most part, silent. They don't want to lose their tax exempt status. If they lose that, they'll lose the people's tithes and their money is more important than preaching the truth. There is so much pressure on the church today to accept homosexuality as a viable lifestyle and many segments of the church has fallen for the lies of "God made me this way." That is a lie from the pit of hell. His word says that this lifestyle is an abomination to Him. He is not going to create someone that is an abomination to Him. Even sex outside of marriage has been accepted by some segments of

Bring America Back To Her Religious Roots

Chapter 17 – The Fight

the church. They have fallen for the lie that everybody does it; God designed it so it must be OK. The only problem is, nowhere in scripture does it condone sex outside of marriage, or living together outside of marriage, or homosexuality.

This kind of mentality makes a person feel good about their sin. They should feel terrible about their sin, but preachers today don't want to make their congregations feel uncomfortable. One preacher a few years back said the worse thing a preacher could do was remind the sinner of their sin. Then a few years later, he fired his son because 'he preached from the Bible.' The church does not show the power and strength of God's Word when they don't stand for anything. We seem to act like we are trying to hold back darkness with our own strength. We have forgotten that we have a higher power that is on our side. Zechariah 4:6 *". . . Not by might, nor by power, but by my spirit, saith the LORD of hosts."*

Chapter 18

The Finale

Bring America Back To Her Religious Roots

Chapter 18 – The Finale

Too many of today's so-called historians try to put religion behind closed doors like it is something to be ashamed of. Paul stated in **Romans 1:16** *"For I am not ashamed of the gospel of Christ: for it is the power of God unto salvation to everyone that believeth; to the Jew first, and also to the Greek."* Why are the preachers today afraid to preach the truth? When they stand before God they will have to answer to Him as to why they preached another gospel. Paul spoke of this in **Galatians 1:6** *"I marvel that ye are so soon removed from him that called you into the grace of Christ unto another gospel:"* How easily we are swayed. Those that stand strong on the Word have been labeled racist, bigots and even worse, but when they stand before God, they will be able to say that they preached the truth. When I hear that we have never been a Christian nation and that our Founding Fathers were deists, atheist and agnostics, I wonder why these lies are not confronted. In looking at

Bring America Back To Her Religious Roots

Part 18 – The Finale

historical documents that record who and what our Founding Fathers were and did, it amazes me how these lies are allowed to be taught without confrontation. To just scratch the surface of this historical evidence I want to share with you what some of these so-called deists and atheists did.

John Quincy Adams: Vice-President of the American Bible Society, member of the Massachusetts Bible Society. Elias Boudinot: (President of the Continental Congress)Founder and first President of the American Bible Society, President of the New Jersey Bible Society, member of the American Board of Commissioners for Foreign Missions, member of the Massachusetts Society for Promoting Christian Knowledge.
Alexander Hamilton: (Signer of the Constitution) Proposed formation of the Christian Constitutional Society to spread Christian governments to other nations.
John Jay: (Original Chief Justice of the Supreme Court): President of the American Bible Society, member of the

Bring America Back To Her Religious Roots

Part 18 – The Finale

American Board of Commissioners for Foreign Missions. I could go on for the rest of the 250 Founding Fathers and the story would be the same except for a small handful. NONE can be called atheist. In an article in *American Heritage* authored by Gordon Wood he states: *"The Founding Fathers were at most deists . . . and were a very thin veneer on their society."* According to ALL historical documents, that statement is a lie! In another national article Steve Morris claimed: *"The early presidents and patriots were generally deists or Unitarians, believing in some form of impersonal Providence but rejecting the divinity of Jesus and the relevance of the Bible."* Contemporary works incorrectly claim that Jefferson called himself a deist. Yet historical records are clear that he *never* called himself a deist, but he did call himself a Christian: *"I am a real Christian, that is to say, a disciple of the doctrines of Jesus Christ."*

The definition of deist in the days of our Founding Fathers is

Bring America Back To Her Religious Roots

Part 18 – The Finale

different than today's definition. Benjamin Franklin called himself a deist, but rejected the 'clockmaker' theory of today's deists. He did believe in prayer and he believed that those prayers brought intervention from God. Patrick Henry defended his position as a Christian even in his day: *"The rising greatness of our country . . . is greatly tarnished by the general prevalence of deism which, with me, is but another name for vice and depravity. . . I hear it is said by the deists that I am one of their number; and indeed that some good people think I am no Christian. This thought gives me\ much more pain that the appellation of Tory (being called a traitor), because I think religion infinitely higher importance than politics. . . Being a Christian is a character which I prize far above all this world has or can boast."* John Witherspoon declared: *"Shun, as a contagious pestilence. . . those especially whom you perceive to be infected with the principles of infidelity (denying scripture) or who are enemies to the power of religion. Whoever is an*

Bring America Back To Her Religious Roots

Part 18 – The Finale

avowed enemy of God, I scruple (hesitate) not to call him an enemy to his country."

In 1825 the grandson of Richard Henry Lee, President of the Continental Congress and the man who introduced to Congress the call for American independence, compiled documents of his grandfather which consisted of hand written letters from many of the Founding Fathers, George Washington, Benjamin Rush, and many others. He studied these letters and described this great body of men who founded this nation in these words:

"The wise and great men of those days were not ashamed publicly to confess the Name of our blessed Lord and Savior Jesus Christ! In behalf of the people, as their representatives and rulers, they acknowledged the sublime doctrine of his meditation." Ignoring all the historical evidence is the only way the contemporary historians can bolster their argument for the unfounded separation of church and state that they demand. The Founding Fathers understood the multiple benefits of

Bring America Back To Her Religious Roots

Part 18 – The Finale

religion. They therefore aggressively promoted religion throughout American society. The departure from that practice was facilitated by the laxness of the citizenry in understanding, and the Supreme Court in upholding the Constitutions original intent. When the intent under girding a law is abandoned, then that law can be applied in a manner that is contrary to its intended purpose; the result of that can be devastating. The Supreme Court, in either complete ignorance of our history or because of the agenda they felt should be applied (I believe both), declared: *"A union of government and religion tends to destroy government and to degrade religion."* This is in direct contrast to James Wilson, a signer of the Declaration of Independence AND a signer of the Constitution who *stated "Far from being rivals, religion and law are twin sisters."* Of course what James Wilson meant by "law" was government. We must not let these truths be forgotten. Ronald Reagan warned us *"If we ever forget that we are One Nation Under*

Bring America Back To Her Religious Roots

Part 18 – The Finale

God, then we will be a nation gone under." Will we stand up for what our Founding Fathers fought and died for or will we let it slip through our hands? John Quincy Adams declared *"Posterity: you will never know how much it has cost my generation to preserve your freedom. I hope you will make good use of it."* It is now in our hands. What will you do?

A Prayer for our Nation

Father, we ask You to bless and heal our land. We pray for this nation, that we will humbly and wholeheartedly serve You. We pray that as a nation we shall have no other gods before You; that we will not bow down ourselves before any idol or image; we shall not take Your Name in vain; that we will keep the Sabbath day holy; that we will honor our father and mother; that we shall not kill , steal, commit adultery, or bear false witness against our neighbor; that we will not covet anything that is our neighbors; and that the fear of the Lord would be in all the inhabitants of this nation.

I thank You Father that You are revealing to the hearts and minds of the people of this nation that You are bringing this nation back to its foundational roots. I thank You that whether they be elected or appointed, if they are hindering that process or opposed to Your righteousness, that You are exposing them and removing them. I thank You that with each election between now and the time Jesus returns we will see the ungodly and the unrighteous removed from office and be replaced with godly, righteous, Spirit filled men and women of God.

We pray that as a nation, we will hide Your Word in our hearts, that we might not sin against thee; that we would walk by faith and not by sight; that we would love You with all of our heart, soul, mind and strength, and love our neighbor as ourselves; that we would diligently obey Your voice, and cleave to you; for You are our life and the length of our days, and Father, without You, we can do nothing. Grant our request, according to 2 Chronicles 7:14, in Jesus Name.

Amen

Pastor Roger Anghis

Philippians 4:8

Biographies

Of the Founding Fathers

George Washington

The first child of Augustine Washington (1694–1743) and his second wife, Mary Ball Washington (1708–1789), George Washington was born on their Pope's Creek Estate near present-day Colonial Beach in Westmoreland County, Virginia. According to the Julian calendar, which was in use at the time, Washington was born on February 11, 1731; according to the Gregorian calendar, implemented in 1752, according to the provisions of the Calendar Act 1750, the date was February 22, 1732. Washington's ancestors were from Sulgrave, England; his great-grandfather, John Washington, had immigrated to Virginia in 1657. George's father Augustine was a tobacco planter who later tried his hand in iron-mining ventures.

On January 6, 1759, Washington married the wealthy widow Martha Dandridge Custis. George and Martha never had any children together – his earlier bout with smallpox in 1751 may have made him sterile. Washington may not have been able to admit to his own sterility while privately he grieved over not having his own children. The newlywed couple moved to Mount Vernon, near Alexandria, where he took up the life of a planter and political figure.

After the Battles of Lexington and Concord near Boston in April 1775, the colonies went to war. Washington appeared at the Second Continental Congress in a military uniform, signaling that he was prepared for war. Washington had the

prestige, military experience, charisma and military bearing of a military
leader and was known as a strong patriot. Virginia, the largest colony, deserved recognition, and New England—where the fighting began—realized it needed
Southern support. Washington did not explicitly seek the office of commander and said that he was not equal to it, but there was no serious competition. Congress created the Continental Army on June 14, 1775. Nominated by John Adams of Massachusetts, Washington was then appointed Major General and Commander-in-chief.

The Electoral College elected Washington unanimously as the first president in 1789, and again in the 1792 election; he remains the only president to have received 100 percent of the electoral votes.

Washington reluctantly served a second term. He refused to run for a third, establishing the customary policy of a maximum of two terms for a president.

John Adams

John Adams, Jr., the eldest of three sons, was born on October 30, 1735 (October 19, 1735 Old Style, Julian calendar), in what is now Quincy, Massachusetts (then called the "north precinct" of Braintree, Massachusetts), to John Adams, Sr., and Susanna Boylston Adams. While he did not speak much of his mother later in life, he commonly praised his father and was very close to him as a child. Adams' birthplace is now part of Adams National Historical Park. His father, also named John (1691–1761), was a fifth-generation descendant of Henry Adams, who emigrated from Somerset in England to Massachusetts Bay Colony in about 1638. John Adams, Sr. was a farmer, a Congregationalist (that is, Puritan) deacon, a lieutenant in the militia and a selectman, or town councilman, who supervised schools and roads; Susanna Boylston Adams was a descendant of the Boylstons of Brookline.

Adams first rose to prominence as an opponent of the Stamp Act of 1765, which was imposed by the British Parliament without consulting the American legislatures. Americans protested vehemently that it violated their traditional rights as Englishmen. Popular resistance, he later observed, was sparked by an oft-reprinted sermon of the Boston minister, Jonathan Mayhew, interpreting Romans 13 to elucidate the principle of just insurrection. Massachusetts sent Adams to the first and second

Continental Congresses in 1774 and from 1775 to 1777. In June 1775, with a view of promoting union among the colonies, he nominated George Washington of Virginia as commander-in-chief of the army then assembled around Boston. His influence in Congress was great, and almost from the beginning, he sought permanent separation from Britain. He was appointed to a committee with Thomas Jefferson, Benjamin Franklin, Robert R. Livingston and Roger Sherman, to draft the Declaration of Independence, which was to be ready when congress voted on independence. Congress twice dispatched Adams to represent the fledgling union in Europe, first in 1777, and again in 1779. Accompanied, on both occasions, by his eldest son, John Quincy (who was ten years old at the time of the first voyage), Adams sailed for France aboard the Continental Navy frigate Boston on February 15, 1778.

While Washington won the presidential election of 1789 with 69 votes in the electoral college, Adams came in second with 34 votes and became Vice President. According to David McCullough, what he really might have wanted was to be the first Chief Justice of the Supreme Court of the United States. He presided over the Senate but otherwise played a minor role in the politics of the early 1790s; he was reelected in 1792. Washington seldom asked Adams for input on policy and legal issues during his tenure as vice president.

As President, Adams followed Washington's lead in making the presidency the example of republican values, and stressing civic virtue; he was never implicated in any scandal. Adams continued not just the Washington cabinet but all the major programs of the Washington Administration as well. Adams continued to strengthen the central government, in particular by expanding the navy and army. His economic programs were a continuation of those of Hamilton, who regularly consulted with key cabinet members, especially the powerful Secretary of the Treasury, Oliver Wolcott, Jr. Adams' term was marked by intense disputes over foreign policy, in particular a desire to stay out of the expanding conflict in Europe. Britain and France were at war; Hamilton and the Federalists favored Britain, while Jefferson and the Democratic-Republicans favored France. The French wanted Jefferson to be elected president, and when he wasn't, they became even more belligerent. When Adams entered

office, he realized that he needed to continue Washington's policy of staying out of the European war.
In the closing months of his term Adams became the first president to occupy the new, but unfinished President's Mansion (later known as the White House), beginning November 1, 1800. Since 1800 was not a leap year, he served one less day in office than all other one-term presidents.

Thomas Jefferson

The third of ten children, Thomas Jefferson was born on April 13, 1743 at the family home in Shadwell, Goochland County, Virginia, now part of Albemarle County. His father was Peter Jefferson, a planter and a surveyor. He was of possible Welsh descent, although this remains unclear. His mother was Jane Randolph, daughter of Isham Randolph, a ship's captain and sometime planter. Peter and Jane married in 1739. Thomas Jefferson was little interested and indifferent to his ancestry and he only knew of the existence of his paternal grandfather.

In 1752, Jefferson began attending a local school run by a Scottish Presbyterian minister. At the age of nine, Jefferson began studying Latin, Greek, and French; he learned to ride horses, and began to appreciate the study of nature. He studied under the Reverend James Maury from 1758 to 1760 near Gordonsville, Virginia.

At age 16, Jefferson entered the College of William & Mary in Williamsburg, and first met the law professor George Wythe, who became his influential mentor. For two years he studied mathematics, metaphysics, and philosophy under Professor William Small, who introduced the enthusiastic Jefferson to the writings of the British Empiricists, including John Locke, Francis Bacon, and Isaac Newton.

Jefferson handled many cases as a lawyer in colonial Virginia, and was very active from 1768 to 1773. Jefferson's client list included members of the Virginia's elite families, including members of his mother's family, the Randolphs.

Beside practicing law, Jefferson represented Albemarle County in the Virginia House of Burgesses beginning on May 11, 1769 and ending June 20, 1775.

Jefferson served as a delegate to the Second Continental Congress beginning in June 1775, soon after the outbreak of the American Revolutionary War. He sought out John Adams who, along with his cousin Samuel, had emerged as a leader of the convention. Jefferson and Adams established a lifelong friendship; Adams ensured that Jefferson was appointed to the five-man committee to write a declaration in support of the resolution of independence.

The Declaration was the "core of [Jefferson]'s seductive appeal across the ages". After working for two days to modify the document, as they wanted it to appeal to the population in Great Britain as well as the US, on July 4, 1776, Congress ratified the Declaration of Independence and distributed the document. Historians have considered it to be one of Jefferson's major achievements; the preamble is considered an enduring statement of human rights that has inspired people around the world. Its second sentence is the following:

We hold these truths to be self-evident, that all men are created equal, that they are endowed by their Creator with certain unalienable Rights, that among these are Life, Liberty and the pursuit of Happiness

Working closely with Aaron Burr of New York, Jefferson rallied his party, attacking the new taxes especially, and ran for the Presidency in 1800. Before the passage of the Twelfth Amendment, a problem with the new union's electoral system arose.

Hamilton convinced his party that Jefferson would be a lesser political evil than Burr and that such scandal within the electoral process would undermine the new constitution. On February 17, 1801, after thirty-six ballots, the House elected Jefferson President and Burr Vice President.

Jefferson owed his election victory to the South's inflated

number of Electors, which counted slaves under the three-fifths compromise.

Jefferson had sent James Monroe and Robert R. Livingston to Paris in 1802 to try to buy the city of New Orleans and adjacent coastal areas. At Jefferson's request, Pierre Samuel du Pont de Nemours, a French nobleman who had close ties with both Jefferson and Napoleon, also helped negotiate the purchase with France. Napoleon offered to sell the entire Louisiana Territory for a price of $15 million, which Treasury Secretary Albert Gallatin financed easily. Jefferson acted contrary to his usual requirement of explicit

Constitutional authority, and the Federalists criticized him for acting without that authority, but most thought that this opportunity could not be missed.

Jefferson had an avid interest in the sciences and had long entertained ideas of exploring the American frontier before Louisiana was purchased from France. As such Jefferson was a member of the American Philosophical Society, founded in Philadelphia in 1743 by Benjamin Franklin, and served as its President from 1797 to 1815. By the turn of the 19th century, the society was well established and staffed, and equipped for research. Jefferson made use of its resources by sending Meriwether Lewis to Philadelphia in 1803 for instruction at the Society in botany, mathematics, surveying, astronomy, chemistry and map making, among other subjects.

Ideas for a national institution for military education were circulated during the American Revolution. It wasn't until 1802 when Jefferson, following the advice of George Washington, John Adams and others,[99] finally convinced Congress to authorize the funding and building of the United States Military Academy at West Point on the Hudson River in New York. On March 16, 1802, Jefferson signed the Military Peace Establishment Act, directing that a corps of engineers be established and "stationed at West Point in the state of New York, and shall constitute a Military Academy."

Jefferson' health began to deteriorate by July 1825, and by June 1826 he was confined to bed. His death was from a combination of illnesses and conditions including uremia, severe diarrhea, and pneumonia.[129] Jefferson died on July 4, 1826, the fiftieth

anniversary of the Declaration of Independence, and a few hours
before John Adams.

James Madison

James Madison, Jr. was born at Belle Grove Plantation near Port Conway, Virginia on March 16, 1751. He grew up as the oldest of twelve children. His father, James Madison, Sr. (1723–1801), was a tobacco planter who grew up on an estate in Orange County, Virginia, which he inherited upon reaching maturity. He later acquired more property and, with 5,000 acres (2,000 ha), became the largest landowner and a leading citizen of Orange County.

In 1769, he enrolled at the College of New Jersey, now Princeton University. Through diligence and long hours of study that may have damaged his health, Madison graduated in 1771. His studies there included Latin, Greek, science, geography, mathematics, rhetoric, and philosophy. Great emphasis also was placed on speech and debate. After graduation, Madison remained at Princeton to study Hebrew and political philosophy under university president John Witherspoon before returning to Montpelier in the spring of 1772.

Madison served in the Virginia state legislature (1776–79) and became known as a protégé of Thomas Jefferson. As a young man, Madison witnessed the persecution of Baptist preachers arrested for preaching without a license from the established

Anglican Church. He worked with the preacher Elijah Craig on constitutional guarantees for religious liberty in Virginia. Working on such cases helped form his ideas about religious freedom. He attained prominence in Virginia politics, helping to draft the Virginia Statute for Religious Freedom. It disestablished the Church of England and disclaimed any power of state compulsion in religious matters.

As a delegate to the Continental Congress (1780–83), Madison was considered a legislative workhorse and a master of parliamentary coalition building. He was elected to the Virginia House of Delegates for a second time from 1784 to 1786. Madison was crucial in persuading George Washington to attend the Constitutional Convention, since he knew how important Washington would be to its ultimate adoption. Madison was one of the first delegates to arrive, and while waiting for the convention to begin Madison wrote what became known as the Virginia Plan. The Virginia Plan was submitted at the opening of the convention, and the work of the convention quickly became to amend the Virginia Plan and to fill in the gaps. Though the Virginia Plan was an outline rather than a draft of a possible constitution, and though it was heavily changed during the debate (especially by John Rutledge and James Wilson in the Committee of Detail) its use at the convention has led many to call Madison the "Father of the Constitution". During the course of the Convention he spoke over two hundred times.

The Constitution as it came out of the convention in Philadelphia had to be ratified. It would not be ratified by state legislatures but by special conventions called in each state to decide that sole question of ratification.[24] Madison was a leader in the ratification effort. He, Alexander Hamilton and John Jay wrote the Federalist Papers, a series of 85 newspaper articles published in New York to explain how the proposed Constitution would work, mainly by responding to criticisms from anti-federalists. They were also published in book form and became a virtual debater's handbook for the supporters of the Constitution in the ratifying conventions.

Madison is considered the Father of the Bill of Rights. Without his influence to establish them they might not have been written. He helped establish the Democrat-Republican Party with Thomas Jefferson. He was Secretary of State from 1801-1809 under Thomas Jefferson.

By 1809 the Federalist party had almost completely disappeared, and its former members (such as John Quincy Adams, Madison's ambassador to Russia) had joined Madison's Democratic-Republican party. Madison served two terms 1809-1817 as President.

James Monroe

James Monroe was born on April 28, 1758, in a wooded area of Westmoreland County, Virginia. The site is marked and is one mile from what is known today as Monroe Hall, Virginia. Monroe's father, Spence Monroe (1727–1774) was a moderately prosperous planter who also learned the carpentry trade. His mother, Elizabeth Jones Monroe (1730–1774), married Spence Monroe in 1752. His paternal great-grandfather immigrated to America from Scotland in the mid-17th century.

Monroe enrolled in the College of William and Mary. However in 1774, the atmosphere on the Williamsburg campus was not conducive to study, and the prospect of rebellion against King George charged most of the students, including Monroe, with patriotic fervor. The following spring, Monroe dropped out of college and joined the 3rd Virginia Regiment in the Continental Army. In June 1775, after the battles of Lexington and Concord, Monroe joined 24 older men in raiding the arsenal at the Governor's Palace. The 200 muskets and 300 swords they appropriated helped arm the Williamsburg militia. The following spring, Monroe dropped out of college and joined the Continental army. He never returned to earn a degree.

Between 1780 and 1783, he studied law under Thomas Jefferson.

Monroe was elected to the Virginia House of Delegates in 1782.

After serving for the Continental legislature he was elected to the Fourth Continental Congress in November of 1783. He was also elected to and served in the Fifth and Sixth Congresses, serving for a total of three years where he finally retired from that office by the rule of rotation.

Monroe resigned his Senate seat after being appointed Minister to France in 1794. As ambassador, Monroe secured the release of Thomas Paine when he was arrested for his opposition to the execution of Louis XVI on the condition that he be sent to America.

He managed to free all the Americans held in French prisons, Out of office, Monroe returned to practicing law in Virginia until elected governor there as a Republican, his first term serving from 1799 to 1802. He was reelected Virginia's governor four times.

President Jefferson sent Monroe to France to assist Robert R. Livingston to negotiate the Louisiana Purchase. Monroe was then appointed Minister to the Court of St. James (Britain) from 1803 to 1807. In 1806 he negotiated a treaty with Britain, known as the Monroe–Pinkney Treaty.

Monroe returned to the Virginia House of Delegates and was elected to another term as governor in 1811, but only served four months. He became Secretary of State in April of that year. He had little to do with the War of 1812, as President Madison and the War Hawks in Congress were dominant. The war went very badly, and when the British burned the capitol building on August 24, 1814, Madison removed John Armstrong as Secretary of War and turned to Monroe for help, appointing him Secretary of War on September 27. Monroe resigned as Secretary of State on October 1, but no successor was ever appointed, so he continued doing the work. Thus from October 1, 1814, to February 28, 1815, Monroe effectively held both cabinet posts.

Monroe informed Congress in March 1822 that permanent stable governments had been established in the United Provinces of La Plata (present-day Argentina), Chile, Peru, Colombia and Mexico. Adams, under Monroe's supervision, wrote the instructions for the ministers (ambassadors) to these new countries. They declared that the policy of the United States was to uphold republican institutions and to seek treaties of commerce on a most-favored-nation basis. This ultimately became known as the Monroe Doctrine.

John Quincy Adams

John Quincy Adams was born to John Adams and his wife Abigail Adams in what is now Quincy, Massachusetts. The John Quincy Adams Birthplace is now part of Adams National Historical Park and open to the public. He was named for his mother's maternal grandfather, Colonel John Quincy, after whom Quincy, Massachusetts, is named. Adams first learned of the Declaration of Independence from the letters his father wrote his mother from the Second Continental Congress in Philadelphia. In 1779, Adams began a diary that he kept until just before he died in 1848. The massive fifty volumes are one of the most extensive collections of first-hand information from the period of the early republic, and are widely cited by modern historians.

Much of Adams' youth was spent accompanying his father overseas. John Adams served as an American envoy to France from 1778 until 1779 and to the Netherlands from 1780 until 1782, and the younger Adams accompanied his father on these journeys. Adams acquired an education at institutions such as Leiden University. For nearly three years, at the age of 14, he accompanied Francis Dana as a secretary on a mission to Saint Petersburg, Russia, to obtain recognition of the new United States. He spent time in Finland, Sweden, and Denmark and, in

1804, published a travel report of Silesia. During these years overseas, Adams became fluent in French and Dutch and became familiar with German and other European languages. He entered Harvard College and graduated in 1787 with a Bachelor of Arts degree, Phi Beta Kappa.

John Quincy Adams was elected a member of the Massachusetts State Senate in April 1802. In November 1802 he ran as a Federalist for the United States House of Representatives and lost.

The Massachusetts General Court elected Adams as a Federalist to the U.S. Senate soon after, and he served from March 4, 1803, until 1808, when he broke with the Federalist Party. Adams, as a Senator, had supported the Louisiana Purchase and Jefferson's Embargo Act, actions which made him very unpopular with Massachusetts Federalists. The Federalist-controlled Massachusetts Legislature chose a replacement for Adams on June 3, 1808, several months early.

Adams served as Secretary of State in the Cabinet of President James Monroe from 1817 until 1825. Typically, his views concurred with those espoused by Monroe. As Secretary of State, he negotiated the Adams–Onís Treaty (also known as the Florida Treaty), the Treaty of 1818, and wrote the Monroe Doctrine. Many historians believe that he was one of the greatest secretaries of state in American history.

Adams had a strong base in New England. His opponents included John C. Calhoun, William H. Crawford, Henry Clay and the hero of New Orleans, Andrew Jackson. During the campaign Calhoun dropped out, and Crawford fell ill giving further support to the other candidates. When Election Day arrived, Andrew Jackson won, although narrowly, pluralities of the popular and electoral votes, but not the necessary majority of electoral votes.

Under the terms of the Twelfth Amendment, the presidential election fell to the House of Representatives, which was to choose from the top three candidates: Jackson, Adams, and Crawford. Clay had come in fourth place and thus was not on the ballot, but he retained considerable power and influence as Speaker of the House.

Clay's personal dislike for Jackson and the similarity of his American System to Adams' position on tariffs and internal improvements caused him to throw his support to Adams, who was elected by the House on February 9, 1825, on the first ballot.

The Adams administration's record was mixed, as it recorded some domestic policy achievements, as well as some minor foreign policy achievements. He supported internal improvements (roads, ports and canals), a national university, and federal support for the arts and sciences. He favored a high tariff to encourage the building of factories, and restricted land sales to slow the movement west.

Andrew Jackson

Jackson was born on March 15, 1767. His parents were Scots-Irish colonists Andrew and Elizabeth Hutchinson Jackson, Presbyterians who had emigrated from Ireland two years earlier. Jackson received a sporadic education in the local "old-field" school. In 1781, he worked for a time in a saddle-maker's shop. Later, he taught school and studied law in Salisbury, North Carolina. In 1787, he was admitted to the bar, and moved to Jonesborough, in what was then the Western District of North Carolina. This area later became the Southwest Territory (1790), the precursor to the state of Tennessee.

During the American Revolutionary War, Jackson, at age thirteen, joined a local militia as a courier. His eldest brother, Hugh, died from heat exhaustion during the Battle of Stono Ferry, on June 20, 1779. Jackson and his brother Robert were captured by the British and held as prisoners; they nearly starved to death in captivity. When Jackson refused to clean the boots of a British officer, the officer slashed at the youth with a sword, leaving Jackson with scars on his left hand and head, as well as an intense hatred for the British. While imprisoned, the brothers contracted smallpox.

Jackson began his legal career in Jonesborough, now northeastern Tennessee. Though his legal education was scanty, he knew enough to be a country lawyer on the frontier. Since he

was not from a distinguished family, he had to make his career by his own merits; soon he began to prosper in the rough-and-tumble world of frontier law. Most of the actions grew out of disputed land-claims, or from
assault and battery. In 1788, he was appointed Solicitor (prosecutor) of the Western District and held the same position in the government of the Territory South of the River Ohio after 1791.

Jackson was elected as a delegate to the Tennessee constitutional convention in 1796. When Tennessee achieved statehood that year, Jackson was elected its U.S. Representative. The following year, he was elected U.S. Senator as a Democratic-Republican, but he resigned within a year. In 1798, he was appointed a judge of the Tennessee Supreme Court, serving until 1804.

Jackson was appointed commander of the Tennessee militia in 1801, with the rank of colonel. He was later elected major general of the Tennessee militia in 1802.

Jackson's service in the War of 1812 against the United Kingdom was conspicuous for bravery and success. When British forces threatened New Orleans, Jackson took command of the defenses, including militia from several western states and territories. He was a strict officer but was popular with his troops. They said he was "tough as old hickory" wood on the battlefield, and he acquired the nickname of "Old Hickory". In the Battle of New Orleans on January 8, 1815

Jackson won the presidential election of 1828 against John Quincy Adams. Both candidates were rhetorically attacked in the press, which reached a low point when the press accused Jackson's wife Rachel of bigamy. Though the accusation was true, as were most personal attacks leveled against him during the campaign, it was based on events that occurred many years prior (1791 to 1794). Jackson said he would forgive those who insulted him, but he would never forgive the ones who attacked his wife. Rachel died suddenly on December 22, 1828, before his inauguration, and was buried on Christmas Eve.

In the 1832 presidential election, Jackson easily won reelection as the candidate of the Democratic Party against Henry Clay, of the National Republican Party, and William Wirt, of the Anti-Masonic Party. Jackson jettisoned Vice President John C.

Calhoun because of his support for nullification and involvement in the Petticoat affair, replacing him with longtime confidant Martin Van Buren of New York.